Table of Contents

Introduction

My story has started a long time before I decided to be slim. Ever since childhood, I was overweight. During the teen time, my situation wasn't so deplorable. I am grateful to my family because they always accepted me as I am. But it wasn't enough for me because all around hated me. At the age of 15, I understood that I am unshapely girl. I was in graduation class, my weight has already exceeded 270 lbs. I felt like I am a giant cow who couldn't fit into any sexy dress for a prom party. My parents have never been worried about weight, they just repeated all the time "you are an angel, you are beautiful". I knew that it wasn't true, in the mirror I saw plum girl. After graduating from school, I became very depressed. All my troubles I jammed with tones of chocolate and Coke.

One sunny day I firmly decided for myself - enough for me! I don't want to live like that anymore. I will be changed. I had made the "wish map", where I was slim and smiling, and started to do sports and eat fewer sweets and sparkling drinks. I couldn't say that it wasn't successful but I didn't get the desired result. I wanted everything at once, so I even practiced fasting. I could drink water and vegetable smoothies for 2-3 days. But it all ended with me breaking down and gaining even more weight. At that time, I already started having health problems. I could not walk for a long time, I was haunted by headaches, pain in my stomach, as well as bad breath.

I decided to go to the doctor and do a comprehensive analysis of the whole body. When my doctor looked at my tests, he advised going to a nutritionist. This time I discovered a ketogenic diet. The doctor didn't prescribe something special. It was a certain diet and simple physical exercises every day. But I have to eat a lot of proteins, and almost no vegetables (I hated them at that time). I couldn't believe that everything is so easy! But I didn't lose faith and clearly followed the doctor's instructions. After a week of keto life, I did not see significant results, but after 2 weeks the arrows of the scales showed -8 lbs. During the year of keto lifestyle, my weight dropped by 83 lbs and my health became better. I cried with happiness! Finally, I did it! This is just a miracle! Now I am a wife, mom, and just happy woman!

I wrote this book to help people like me. To those who still think that they are hopeless! I am sure that this diet will change your way of thinking and make a big difference in your life. I am the greatest example that nothing is impossible. You should know that losing weight is not only restrictions and starving. The real-life on keto diet exists and this book proves it! Our mind and our body are omnipotent! They know well what we need! Each of us should be dropkicked to take the path of a happy life! I strongly believe that this book will be a guide and silver lining in a better version of you!

What to Eat and Avoid on the Keto Diet

Meat and poultry

Actually, it is the primary type of food for the Keto diet. It contains 0% of carbs and is rich in potassium, selenium, zinc, and B vitamins. Grass-fed meat and poultry are the most beneficial. It caused by high omega 3 fats and antioxidants content. Bear in mind that Keto diet is a high-fat diet and high consumption of proteins can cause to harder getting of ketosis.

What to eat	Enjoy occasionally	What to avoid
• chicken • duck • goose • ground beef • lamb • ostrich • partridge • pheasant • pork • quail • turkey • venison	• bacon • ham • low-fat meat, such as skinless chicken breast • sausage	• breaded meats • processed meats

Dairy

High-fat dairy products are awesome for the keto diet. They are calcium-rich full-fat dairy product is nutritious and can make you full longer. Milk lovers should restrict or even cross out this product from the daily meal plan. It is allowed only 1 tablespoon of milk in your drink per day but doesn't abuse it daily.

What to eat	What to avoid
• butter • cheese (soft and hard) • full-fat yogurt • heavy cream • sour cream	• fat-free yogurt • low-fat cheese • milk • skim milk • skim mozzarella • sweetened yogurt

Eggs

This is the most wholesome food in the world. Use them everywhere you want! Containing less than one gram of carbohydrates, eggs are a wonderful food for the keto lifestyle. Eating eggs reducing the risk of heart disease and save your eyes health.

Note: free-range eggs are healthier options for the keto diet.

What to avoid	
• chicken eggs • duck eggs	• ostrich eggs • quail eggs

- goose eggs

Fish and Seafood

Fatty fish as salmon is beneficial for the keto diet. Small fish like sardines, herring, etc. are less in toxins. The best option for a keto diet is wild-caught seafood; it has a higher number of omega 3 fats.

Scientifically proved that frequent eating of fish improves mental health.

What to eat		What to avoid
• catfish	• prawns	• breaded fish
• clams	• salmon	
• cod	• sardines	
• crab	• scallops	
• halibut	• shrimp	
• herring	• snapper	
• lobster	• swordfish	
• mackerel	• tilapia	
• Mahi Mahi	• trout	
• mussels	• tuna	
• oysters		

Nuts and Seeds

These products are heart-healthy and fiber-rich. Nevertheless, eat nuts and seeds as a snack is a bad idea. As usual, the amount of eaten food can be much more than allowed. Nuts like cashews are very insidious and contain a lot of carbohydrates. Replace them with macadamia or pecan.

What to eat		What to avoid
• almonds	• peanuts	• cashews
• chia seeds	• pecans	• pistachio
• flaxseeds	• pumpkin seeds	• chocolate-covered nuts
• hazelnuts	• walnuts	• nut butter (sweetened)
• nut butter (unsweetened)	• macadamia nuts	

Oils and fats

It is the main component of the keto-friendly sauces and dressings.

Olive oil and coconut oil are highly recommending for everyone who decided to follow the keto diet. They are almost perfect it their fatty acid composition. Avoid artificial trans fats which are poison for our body. This type of fats, as usual, used in French fries, margarine, and crackers.

What to eat	What to avoid
• avocado oil	• grapeseed oil
• coconut oil	• canola oil
• hazelnut oil	• cottonseed oil

• olive oil	• hydrogenated oils
• pumpkin seed oil	• margarine
• sesame oil	• peanut oil
• walnut oil	• soybean oil
	• safflower oil
	• processed vegetable oils

Vegetables

Keto diet cannot work without vegetables, but their usage should be in moderation. Starchy vegetables such as potatoes, sweet potatoes, etc. are deadly for our body and will not bring anything more than overweight. At the same time, vegetables that are low in carbs, are rich in antioxidants and can protect the body from free radicals that damage our cells.

What to eat		What to avoid
• asparagus	• mushrooms	• carrots
• avocado	• olives	• corn
• broccoli	• onions	• beets
• cabbage	• tomatoes	• butternut squash
• cauliflower	• peppers	• parsnips
• celery	• spinach	• potatoes (both sweet and regular)
• cucumber	• zucchini	• pumpkin
• eggplant	• other nonstarchy vegetables	• turnips
• leafy greens		• yams
• lettuce		• yuca
		• other starchy vegetables

Fruits

This type of food is high in carbs that's why they should be limited while keto diet. Besides this, almost all fruits are high in glucose and can enhance blood sugar.

Enjoy occasionally	What to avoid	
• lemons	• apples	• peaches
• pomegranates	• bananas	• pears
• limes	• grapefruits	• pineapple
	• limes	• plums
	• mango	• dried fruits
	• oranges	

Berries

If you are looking for how to substitute fruits, this is your godsend. Berries contain up to 12 grams of net carbs per 3.5 ounces serving. They are high in fiber and can maintain the health of your body and fight with diseases. Note consumption of a huge amount of berries can be harmful.

Enjoy occasionally	What to avoid
• blackberries	• cherries
• blueberries	• grapes
• raspberries	• melon
• strawberries	• watermelon

Beans and legumes

There are no ingredients in this food group that would be healthy for a keto diet. Beans and legumes contain fewer carbs in comparison with root vegetables such as potatoes; nevertheless, this type of carbohydrates fastly adds up.

What to avoid	
• black beans	• navy beans
• chickpeas	• peas
• kidney beans	• pinto beans
• lentils	• soybeans

Condiments

Condiments can make any type of meal awesome. Even a piece of meat will turn into the masterpiece with them. There are only a few products which are better to avoid; nevertheless, nowadays, you can find keto-friendly substitutors in a supermarket.

One more hot tip: putting hot pepper in your meal will reduce the amount of salt you need and make the taste of the dish more saturated.

What to eat	What to avoid
• herbs and spices	• BBQ sauce
• lemon juice	• hot sauces
• mayonnaise with no added sugar	• ketchup
• salad dressings with no added sugar	• maple syrup
• salt and pepper	• salad dressings with added sugar
• vinegar	• sweet dipping sauces
	• tomato sauce

Grain products

Actually, it is needless to say that all grains are forbidden and can't be eaten if you want to achieve ketosis. Grains contain complex carbohydrates that have a feature to be absorbed slower than simple carbohydrates. For better understanding, if the food has keto-friendly carbs, look at the number of starch and sugar. Their number should be minimum.

What to avoid	
• baked goods	• muesli
• bread	• oats
• cereal	• pasta
• corn	• pizza
• crackers	• popcorn
• flour	• rice
• granola	• wheat

Beverages

A variety of keto drinks may shock you. Probably you know that the best beverage for a keto diet is water. Nevertheless, in order to brighten up a little gray everyday life of keto lovers, the consumption of alcoholic beverages is allowed in moderation. For instance, pure forms of alcohol, such as gin, vodka, or tequila can be drunk once per week. They contain zero amounts of carbs. Avoid all sweetened beverages; they are a priori high carbohydrate.

What to eat	Enjoy occasionally	What to avoid
• almond milk • bone broth • coffee (unsweetened) • flax milk • tea (unsweetened) • water (still and sparkling)	• dry wine • hard liquor • vodka • other low carb alcoholic drinks	• alcoholic drinks (sweetened) • beer • cider • coffee (sweetened) • fruit juice • soda • sports drinks • smoothies • tea (sweetened) • wines (sweet)

Sweets

Cakes and cookies cannot help in losing weight in any diet. As for keto, here everything is strict with this. You should try to avoid sugar and sweeteners in any form. Moreover, sweets negatively affect blood sugar and insulin levels.

Enjoy occasionally	What to avoid	
• erythritol • stevia • sucralose	• artificial sweeteners • buns • candy • cakes • chocolate • cookies • custard	• ice cream • pastries • pies • pudding • sugar • tarts

Others

Fast food and processed food contain a huge amount of stabilizers and harmful carbohydrates. The main rule of the Keto diet is avoiding sugar. 99,9% of such food contains harmful sugars. The existence of which in the body negates the achievement of ketosis.

What to avoid
• fast food • processed foods

TOP 10 Air Fryer Tips

1. Make your air fryer hot before cooking.

To ensure the perfect taste of the final dish, preheat the air fryer basket. Some models of air fryer have a preheating mode (you can use it) or just choose the needed mode, temperature and allow the air fryer to run for 2-3 minutes. After this, put the food inside the basket.

2. Add a small amount of water for cooking the fatty food.

Fatty food such as bacon, meatballs, lard, etc. can cause smoke while cooking. To avoid this, add a small amount of water at the beginning of cooking. Doing this you will reach the succulent taste of the meal and get the delicious gravy besides.

3. Grease the air fryer basket with fat or brush with oil from inside for most meals.

Such food as vegetables, lean meat, or seafood doesn't have natural fat. It is recommended to add oil/fat during cooking to prevent stickiness. This trick will also help to reach the crispy crust.

4. Do not overload your air fryer.

To get the crispy and browned crust, ensure that you don't overcrowd the air fryer basket. Put the ingredients in the one layer; it will help to cook the meal gradually and faster. At the same time for getting a soft crust and tender taste, put the ingredients in a few layers and shake them during cooking.

5. Shake the air fryer basket for the perfect crust.

Shake the ingredients in the air fryer during cooking for two-three times. This trick will help to cook the meal gradually and prevent the overturning.

6. Use oil spray rather than liquid oil.

Adding the less amount of oil during cooking will make the meal healthier and crunchier in comparison with deep-fry cooking.

7. Make more space for large items.

To be sure that your succulent pieces of meat are well-cooked, cook them in one layer and with much space from each other. Don't forget to flip the meal during frying.

8. Use the foil during cooking for easier cleaning.

Place the baking foil in the bottom of the air fryer and only after this, put all ingredients inside; after cooking just threw the used baking foil in rubbish and wipe the air fryer with a paper towel.

9. Never clean the air fryer in the dishwasher.

Each of us strives to keep kitchen equipment clean. It is very easier to care about the air fryer. The equipment can be cleaned with regular water and detergent. The washing of air fryer in the air fryer can damage it.

10. Baking with an air fryer is possible!

Don't restrict yourself in cooking the culinary masterpieces. Don't be afraid of experiments. An air fryer can even replace an ordinary stove. It can cook everything from hard-boiled eggs to cakes. All you need is to buy additional molds for your type of air fryer. You can find a lot of accessories for the air fryer in any online shop.

Top 10 Keto Diet Tips

1. Combine together Keto and Intermittent fasting.

Intermittent fasting (IF) is the right way to get ketosis. It gives your body additional benefits.

Scientists showed that connection keto diet and intermittent fasting can up the results which can give only strict following of the keto diet.

IF means not eating and drinking during a determined amount of time. It is recommended to separate your day into a building phase (BP) and cleansing phase(CP); where the building phase is the time between the first and last time of eating (first-last); and cleansing is the opposite time (last-first). Start from 14-hours CP and 11-hours BP. Continue like this till your body adapts to the new daily plan. It can take 2-3 days. The first days will be the hardest but then you will feel relief and you can safely proceed to the next stage where BP turns into 5 hours and CP - into 19 hours.

According to research, women get the highest benefits of IF. It is possible to get rid of adrenal fatigue, hypothyroid, and hormonal imbalance.

2. Staying hydrated is essential.

Our body is 60% water. Water ensures the normal digestion of food and the absorption of nutrients from the intestines. If there is not enough water in the body, there will be discomfort in the abdomen and constipation. Drinking water is important even if you are not on keto.

The kidneys filter 5,000 ounces of blood per day so that the result is 50 ounces of urine. For the normal elimination of toxins and waste substances, you need to drink at least 50 ounces of water per day, but preferably more.

Many people face the problem of unwillingness to drink water. The best way to prevent dehydration and all its unpleasant consequences is to put a bottle or cup of water on the table and take a sip every time you look at the water. If you realize that you are thirsty, then eliminate thirst in time.

Regular drinking of the right amount of water for 1 week will become a habit and you will not be able to live differently.

3. Salt isn't harmful.

Salt plays an important role in complex metabolic processes. It is part of the blood, lymph, saliva, tears, gastric juice, bile - that is, all the fluids of our body. Any fluctuations in the salt content in the blood plasma lead to serious metabolic disorders

When fewer carbohydrates enter the body, insulin levels drop. Less insulin circulating in the body leads to secrete excess water in the kidneys instead of holding it. It means that salt and other important minerals and electrolytes are washed out of the body.

Replenish salt is possible by eating bone broths, cucumbers, celeriac, salty keto nuts, and seeds.

The best salts for keto diet are 2 types of salt. Pink salt has a more saturated, saltier taste, and contains calcium, magnesium, and potassium. Sea salt is simply evaporated seawater. The crystals of sea salt are slightly larger than iodized salt, and it has a stronger aroma. It contains potassium, magnesium, sulfur, phosphorus, and zinc.

4. Sport is important.

It is proved that physical activity improves the health of the whole body in general and accelerates metabolism. When we do sport, the first thing is we get rid of carbohydrates, and only then we burn fats.

On a keto diet, even minimal physical activity contributes to the rapid decomposition of fats. You simply don't have glucose (carbohydrates) and any load breaks down fats. The most effective workouts on an empty stomach. Sports during keto are very comfortable. You do not feel hungry and can play sports without breakdowns and overeating. Your stamina is significantly increased. If the protein is correctly calculated, you don't lose muscle mass with a calorie deficit.

The combination of three types of workouts gives the best result for health, weight dynamics, and even mood! These are workouts, aerobic, and stretching. Start with small loads every day and increase it as you can. Do not forget to take measurements of your body to monitor the result!

5. Reduce stress.

Sometimes, observing all the postulates of the keto lifestyle, ketosis does not occur or occurs very slowly. In 99 cases, it happens due to the level of stress in your life. Thus, the hormone cortisol rises, the sympathetic nervous system is stimulated.

Cortisol is produced in response to any stress, even the most minor. How does it happen?

Cortisol "eats" our muscles to turn them into glucose, it catabolizes bones, which is fraught with osteoporosis, causes increased appetite, and suppresses immunity. It also causes increased production of glucose and insulin, and exactly this stops ketosis.

During keto-adaptation (the first 3 weeks), increased cortisol is produced, because the usual energy, glucose, ceases to flow into the body, and it turns on the "self-preservation mode".

It is very important at first to minimize stress from the outside, then everything will normalize.

You should be able to switch from stimulation of the sympathetic nervous system to parasympathetic. Stimulation of the parasympathetic nervous system contributes to the restoration and accumulation of energy resources. This can be achieved by a simple 15 minutes' meditation. The time when you cannot be interrupted.

6. Sleep above all!

Sleep and stress are two interconnected components. Lack of sleep leads to increased stress. Consequently, stress hormone levels and blood sugar levels rise and we gain weight very fast.

Doctors recommend an 8-9 hour sleep every day. The best time to fall asleep is before 11 pm. An hour before bedtime, try not to use any gadgets. It is better to spend this time in silence, meditation, listening to calm music or reading a paper book. Thus, we calm the nervous system and set it to sleep. If your stress level per day was high, try to spend more time sleeping. it is the sleep that contributes to our weight loss and getting rid of all diseases. There are some tips to improve your sleep comfort:

- Keep cool in the room. The optimum temperature should not exceed 65-70F.
- Use a black mask for sleeping and earplugs.
- Provide good room ventilation.

7. Don't forget about vegetables.

It is obvious that the main resource of vitamins and minerals is vegetables. You can't cross out them totally from daily meals. Consuming them during the keto diet is very important, but should be in moderation. Starchy vegetables such as sweet potatoes and potatoes are not allowed. Nevertheless, at the same time, you can safely substitute them with broccoli, kale, spinach, white cabbage, Brussels sprouts to your diet. Such vegetables are not only low-carb, but also low-calorie and have a huge number of vitamins, antioxidants, and minerals. They will help you stay full for a long time and protect from eating an extra serving of nuts.

One of the tips of keto coaches is to pamper yourself with low-carb berries once a week. At the same time, it is very important to increase physical activity during this day. Cycling will be just right. All this will fill your body with useful antioxidants and will not add extra pounds.

8. MCT oil is a treasure for a keto diet.

MCT oil is medium-chain triglyceride oil. It practically doesn't require splitting in the small intestine and is absorbed already in the duodenum, going directly to the liver. MCT oil is used by the body as an energy source, which leads to an increase in fat loss. On the other hand, MCT oil isn't deposited in body fat like fatty tissue in comparison with other fatty acids, and it has been shown that it improves thermogenesis, that is, the process during which the body creates heat using excess energy.

MCT oils are good for cooking, especially for baking, frying or grilling. This is due to their high point of "smoke", which means that they are very difficult to oxidize from heat and can withstand high temperatures without losing their original chemical structure at room temperature (losing their useful properties). You can also add MTC oil in keto shakes, coffee, tea, and other keto drinks.

9. Do a kitchen audit

The key to getting ketosis is proper low-carb nutrition. Nevertheless, our brain, knowing that somewhere in the fridge or freezer are a bar of chocolate or a package of vanilla ice cream. So it unconsciously creates situations in which we are obliged to eat them. That's why there are no doubts that one of the best tips is to clean your kitchen and all the shelves from the "seducers". Firstly, write a list of food that is not allowed during the diet, and then one by one throw away everything that is on your list. It may seem too radical right away. But just know that all this will help you completely switch to keto life faster and less stressfully for your body. Also, you can make a list of all you have in the fridge and stick this sheet of paper on the fridge. Doing this you will not eat extra snacks during the day.

10. Keep food near you.

Our life is full of events and sometimes we just don't have time to cook. We have a choice to buy high carbohydrate food in the shop or cook the right food by ourselves. All of this needs extra time. That's why you should always have a "healthy snack" with you. No matter what it is. It can be fat bombs, seeds, or nuts. If you have more time, make the keto salads, or find the keto fruits such as avocado and cook the spreads and dips. But bear in mind, you shouldn't cook much in advance. Their expired date is very short. Follow the rule to purchasing all ingredients for snacks in advance, so that they are always in your fridge. This way you can less likely break your diet and get rid of unnecessary overeating. If you don't know what to cook, use the recipe generator which can help you with the meal for your certain list of food.

Breakfast

Spinach Eggs

Preparation time: 8 minutes
Cooking time: 20 minutes
Servings: 4

Ingredients:
- 1 tablespoon avocado oil
- ½ teaspoon chili flakes
- 6 eggs, beaten
- 2 cups spinach, chopped

Directions:
1. In the mixing bowl, mix chili flakes with eggs and spinach.
2. Then brush the air fryer mold with avocado oil. Pour the egg mixture inside and transfer the mold in the air fryer.
3. Cook the meal at 365F for 20 minutes.

Nutrition: calories 103, fat 7.1, fiber 0.5, carbs 1.3, protein 8.8

Cauliflower Frittata

Prep time: 10 minutes
Cooking time: 14 minutes
Servings: 4

Ingredients:
- 4 eggs, beaten
- 1 tablespoon cream cheese
- ½ cup heavy cream
- ½ cup cauliflower, chopped
- ½ teaspoon chili flakes
- ½ teaspoon avocado oil

Directions:
1. In the mixing bowl, mix eggs with cream cheese, heavy cream, and chili flakes.
2. Brush the air fryer basket with avocado oil and put the cauliflower inside. Flatten it in one layer.
3. Then pour the egg mixture over the cauliflower and cook the meal at 370F for 14 minutes.

Nutrition: calories 127, fat 10.9, fiber 0.3, carbs 1.5, protein 6.3

Turkey Bake

Preparation time: 10 minutes
Cooking time: 25 minutes
Servings: 2

Ingredients:
- 1-pound ground turkey
- 2 teaspoons avocado oil
- 2 cups of coconut milk
- 1 cup Monterey jack cheese, shredded
- 2 eggs, beaten
- 1 teaspoon ground black pepper

Directions:
1. Brush the baking pan with avocado oil.
2. After this, mix ground turkey with coconut milk, cheese, eggs, and ground black pepper.
3. Put the mixture in the baking pan and flatten gently.
4. Cook the turkey bake at 370F for 25 minutes.

Nutrition: calories 639, fat 52.1, fiber 2.9, carbs 7.5, protein 43.6

Paprika Egg Cups

Prep time: 10 minutes
Cooking time: 3 minutes

Servings: 2

Ingredients:
- 2 eggs
- 1 tablespoon cream cheese
- 1 teaspoon smoked paprika

Directions:
1. Crack the eggs into the ramekins and top them with smoked paprika and cream cheese.
2. Cook the eggs in the air fryer at 400F for 3 minutes.

Nutrition: calories 83, fat 6.3, fiber 0.4, carbs 1.1, protein 6.1

Eggs with Peppers

Preparation time: 5 minutes
Cooking time: 20 minutes
Servings: 4

Ingredients:
- 2 bell peppers, sliced
- 4 eggs, beaten
- 1 teaspoon avocado oil
- ½ teaspoon white pepper

Directions:
1. Brush the air fryer basket with avocado oil.
2. Then mix the bell peppers with white pepper and put inside the air fryer basket.
3. Pour the beaten eggs over the bell peppers and bake the meal at 360F for 20 minutes.

Nutrition: calories 84, fat 4.7, fiber 0.9, carbs 5.1, protein 6.2

Bacon Cups

Prep time: 10 minutes
Cooking time: 10 minutes

Servings: 3

Ingredients:
- 3 eggs
- ½ teaspoon ground paprika
- 3 bacon slices
- 1 teaspoon avocado oil
- 1 teaspoon chives, chopped

Directions:
1. Brush the ramekins with avocado oil.
2. Arrange the bacon slices in every ramekin in the shape of the circle and bake at 370F for 7 minutes.
3. After this, crack the eggs in the center of every ramekin and bake the meal at 365F for 3 minutes more.
4. Sprinkle the cooked eggs with chives and ground paprika.

Nutrition: calories 169, fat 12.6, fiber 0.2, carbs 0.9, protein 12.7

Broccoli Casserole

Preparation time: 10 minutes
Cooking time: 20 minutes
Servings: 4

Ingredients:
- 2 cups broccoli, chopped
- 4 eggs, beaten
- 1 teaspoon chili flakes
- ½ cup Cheddar cheese, shredded
- 1 teaspoon avocado oil

Directions:
1. Brush the air fryer basket with avocado oil from inside.
2. Then mix broccoli, eggs, chili flakes, and cheese in the mixing bowl.
3. Pour the liquid in the air fryer and cook the casserole at 370F for 20 minutes.

Nutrition: calories 137, fat 9.4, fiber 1.2, carbs 3.6, protein 10.4

French Toasts Cups

Prep time: 12 minutes
Cooking time: 9 minutes
Servings: 2

Ingredients:
- 1/3 cup coconut flour
- 1 egg, beaten
- ¼ teaspoon baking powder
- 2 teaspoons Erythritol
- ¼ teaspoon ground cinnamon
- 1 teaspoon mascarpone
- 1 tablespoon butter, softened

Directions:
1. In the mixing bowl, mix coconut flour with egg, baking powder, Erythritol, ground cinnamon, and mascarpone.
2. Then grease the baking cups with butter and pour the coconut flour mixture inside.
3. Bake the meal at 365F for 9 minutes or until the mixture is set.

Nutrition: calories 168, fat 10.3, fiber 8.2, carbs 14.1, protein 5.8

Cheddar Eggs

Preparation time: 5 minutes
Cooking time: 25 minutes
Servings: 4

Ingredients:
- 4 eggs, beaten
- 1 teaspoon avocado oil
- 2 oz Cheddar cheese, shredded

Directions:
1. Brush the ramekins with avocado oil.

2. Then mix eggs with cheese and pour the mixture inside ramekins.
3. Bake the meal at 355F for 25 minutes.

Nutrition: calories 122, fat 9.2, fiber 0.1, carbs 0.6, protein 9.1

Basil Scotch Eggs

Prep time: 15 minutes
Cooking time: 20 minutes
Servings: 4

Ingredients:
- 4 medium eggs, hard-boiled, peeled
- 2 cups ground pork
- 1 teaspoon dried basil
- ½ teaspoon salt
- 2 tablespoons almond flour

Directions:
1. In the mixing bowl, mix ground pork with basil, salt, and almond flour.
2. Then make 4 balls from the meat mixture.
3. Fill every meatball with cooked egg and put it in the air fryer.
4. Cook the meal at 375F for 20 minutes.

Nutrition: calories 199, fat 14, fiber 0.4, carbs 1.1, protein 16.3

Cheese Mix

Preparation time: 10 minutes
Cooking time: 20 minutes
Servings: 6

Ingredients:
- 1 cup of coconut milk
- 1 teaspoon avocado oil
- 2 tablespoons mascarpone
- 1 cup cheddar cheese, shredded
- 3 eggs, beaten

Directions:

1. Brush the air fryer basket with avocado oil.
2. Then mix coconut milk with mascarpone, cheese, and eggs.
3. Pour the liquid in the air fryer basket and cook it at 350F for 20 minutes.

Nutrition: calories 209, fat 18.7, fiber 0.9, carbs 2.8, protein 2.9

Chili Eggs

Prep time: 5 minutes
Cooking time: 6 minutes
Servings: 5

Ingredients:
- 5 eggs
- 1 teaspoon chili flakes
- 1 teaspoon avocado oil

Directions:
1. Brush the air fryer basket with avocado oil and crack the eggs inside.
2. Sprinkle the eggs with chili flakes and bake them at 360F for 6 minutes.

Nutrition: calories 64, fat 4.5, fiber 0.1, carbs 0.4, protein 5.6

Spiced Eggs

Preparation time: 10 minutes
Cooking time: 20 minutes
Servings: 4

Ingredients:
- 8 eggs
- 1 teaspoon dried basil
- 1 teaspoon ground black pepper
- 1 teaspoon dried oregano
- 1 teaspoon avocado oil

Directions:
1. Brush the air fryer basket with avocado oil from inside.

2. Then crack the eggs inside and top them with ground black pepper and dried oregano.
3. Bake the meal at 355F for 20 minutes.

Nutrition: calories 130 fat 9, fiber 0.4, carbs 1.3, protein 11.2

Cheese Muffins

Prep time: 10 minutes
Cooking time: 10 minutes
Servings: 6

Ingredients:
- 1 cup ground chicken
- ½ cup Cheddar cheese, shredded
- 1 teaspoon dried oregano
- ½ teaspoon salt
- 1 tablespoon butter, softened
- 1 teaspoon dried parsley
- 2 tablespoons coconut flour

Directions:
1. Mix all ingredients in the mixing bowl and stir until homogenous.
2. Then pour the muffin mixture in the muffin molds and transfer the molds in the air fryer.
3. Bake the muffins at 375F for 10 minutes.

Nutrition: calories 110, fat 7.1, fiber 1.1, carbs 2, protein 9.5

Eggs with Olives

Preparation time: 5 minutes
Cooking time: 20 minutes
Servings: 4

Ingredients:
- 4 eggs, beaten
- 2 Kalamata olives, sliced
- 1 teaspoon avocado oil
- ½ teaspoon ground paprika

Directions:

1. Brush the air fryer basket with avocado oil and pour the eggs inside.
2. Sprinkle the eggs with ground paprika and top with olives.
3. Bake the meal at 360F for 20 minutes.

Nutrition: calories 68, fat 4.8, fiber 0.2, carbs 0.7, protein 5.6

Cheddar Biscuits

Prep time: 15 minutes
Cooking time: 8 minutes
Servings: 4

Ingredients:
- ½ cup coconut flour
- ¼ cup Cheddar cheese, shredded
- 1 egg, beaten
- 1 tablespoon cream cheese
- 1 tablespoon coconut oil, melted
- ¾ teaspoon baking powder
- ½ teaspoon ground cardamom

Directions:
1. Mix all ingredients in the mixing bowl and knead the dough.
2. Then make 4 biscuits and put them in the air fryer.
3. Cook the meal at 390F for 8 minutes. Shake the biscuits from time to time to avoid burning.

Nutrition: calories 144, fat 9.2, fiber 6.1, carbs 10.9, protein 5.4

Eggplant Spread

Preparation time: 15 minutes
Cooking time: 20 minutes
Servings: 4

Ingredients:
- 3 eggplants
- 1 teaspoon chili flakes

- 1 teaspoon salt
- ½ teaspoon ground black pepper
- 2 tablespoons avocado oil

Directions:
1. Peel the eggplants and rub them with salt.
2. Cook the eggplants in the air fryer at 365F for 20 minutes.
3. Then chop the eggplant and put it in the blender.
4. Add all remaining ingredients and blend the mixture until smooth.

Nutrition: calories 113, fat 1.6, fiber 14.9, carbs 24.8, protein 4.2

Oregano Fish Sticks

Prep time: 15 minutes
Cooking time: 10 minutes
Servings: 4

Ingredients:
- 8 oz cod fillet
- 1 egg, beaten
- 2 tablespoons coconut shred
- 1 teaspoon dried oregano
- ½ teaspoon salt
- 1 teaspoon avocado oil

Directions:
1. Cut the cod fillet into sticks.
2. Then mix salt with dried oregano and coconut shred.
3. Dip the cod sticks in the beaten egg and coat in the coconut shred mixture.
4. Sprinkle the cod sticks with avocado oil and cook in the air fryer at 400F for 10 minutes.

Nutrition: calories 89, fat 4.3, fiber 0.7, carbs 1.4, protein 11.6

Eggs with Brussel Sprouts

Preparation time: 5 minutes
Cooking time: 20 minutes

Servings: 4

Ingredients:
- 1-pound Brussel sprouts, shredded
- 8 eggs, beaten
- 1 teaspoon avocado oil
- 1 teaspoon ground turmeric
- ½ teaspoon salt

Directions:
1. Mix all ingredients and stir until homogenous.
2. Pour the mixture in the air fryer basket and cook at 365F for 20 minutes.

Nutrition: calories 178, fat 9.3, fiber 4.4, carbs 11.4, protein 15

Bacon Bites

Prep time: 10 minutes
Cooking time: 12 minutes
Servings: 4

.

Ingredients:
- 10 oz bacon, chopped
- 1 teaspoon dried dill
- 4 teaspoons cream cheese
- 1 teaspoon dried oregano

Directions:
1. Put the bacon in the air fryer in one layer and bake for 12 minutes at 375F. Shake the bacon from time to time to avoid burning.
2. Then mix bacon with remaining ingredients and make the balls (bites)

Nutrition: calories 397, fat 30.8, fiber 0.2, carbs 1.5, protein 26.6

Almond Milk Bake

Preparation time: 5 minutes
Cooking time: 25 minutes

Servings: 4

Ingredients:
- 2 cups cauliflower, roughly chopped
- 2 ounces Monterey Jack cheese, shredded
- 4 eggs, beaten
- 1 cup organic almond milk
- 1 teaspoon dried oregano

Directions:
1. In the mixing bowl, mix dried oregano with almond milk and eggs.
2. Pour the liquid in the air fryer basket and add cauliflower and cheese.
3. Close the lid and cook the meal at 350F for 25 minutes.

Nutrition: calories 267, fat 23.1, fiber 2.7, carbs 6.7, protein 11.4

Kielbasa Scramble

Prep time: 10 minutes
Cooking time: 8 minutes
Servings: 4

Ingredients:
- 8 eggs, beaten
- 1 teaspoon dried parsley
- 3 oz kielbasa, chopped
- 1 teaspoon coconut oil
- 1 teaspoon dried oregano

Directions:
1. Preheat the air fryer to 385F.
2. Then toss coconut oil in the air fryer basket and melt it.
3. Add kielbasa and cook it for 2 minutes per side.
4. After this, add eggs, parsley, and oregano.
5. Stir the mixture well and cook it for 4 minutes. Stir the meal again.

Nutrition: calories 185, fat 13.7, fiber 0.2, carbs 1.8, protein 13.9

Mozzarella Eggs

Preparation time: 5 minutes
Cooking time: 20 minutes
Servings: 4

Ingredients:
- 1 cup Mozzarella, shredded
- 4 eggs
- 1 teaspoon coconut oil, softened
- ½ teaspoon ground black pepper

Directions:
1. Grease the air fryer basket with coconut oil and crack eggs inside.
2. Sprinkle the eggs with ground black pepper and Mozzarella.
3. Cook the meal at 360F for 20 minutes.

Nutrition: calories 93, fat 6.8, fiber 0.1, carbs 0.8, protein 7.6

Ground Pork Casserole

Prep time: 15 minutes
Cooking time: 25 minutes
Servings: 6

Ingredients:
- 2 jalapeno peppers, sliced
- 2 cups ground pork
- 1 cup Cheddar cheese, shredded
- 1 teaspoon coconut oil
- 1 teaspoon chili flakes
- ½ teaspoon ground turmeric

Directions:
1. Grease the air fryer basket with coconut oil.
2. Then mix ground pork with jalapeno peppers, chili flakes, and ground turmeric.

3. Put the mixture in the air fryer basket and flatten it. Top the mixture with Cheddar cheese.
4. Cook the casserole at 380F for 25 minutes.

Nutrition: calories 395, fat 28.8, fiber 0.2, carbs 0.7, protein 31.6

Tomato Omelet

Preparation time: 5 minutes
Cooking time: 20 minutes
Servings: 4

Ingredients:
- 6 eggs, beaten
- 1 tomato, chopped
- 1 teaspoon coconut oil, melted
- ½ teaspoon dried dill
- ½ teaspoon salt

Directions:
1. Mix eggs with dried dill and salt.
2. Grease the air fryer basket with coconut oil and pour the egg mixture inside.
3. Add chopped tomatoes and cook the omelet for 20 minutes at 365F.

Nutrition: calories 107, fat 7.7, fiber 0.2, carbs 1.2, protein 8.5

Omelet with Herbs de Provence

Prep time: 10 minutes
Cooking time: 18 minutes
Servings: 3

Ingredients:
- 6 eggs, beaten
- 1 tablespoon coconut milk
- 1 teaspoon Herbs de Provence
- 1 teaspoon coconut oil
- 1 oz Parmesan, grated

Directions:
1. Grease the air fryer basket with coconut oil.
2. Mix eggs with coconut oil and Herbs de Provence. Pour the liquid in the air fryer.
3. Then top it with Parmesan and cook the meal at 365F for 18 minutes.

Nutrition: calories 181, fat 13.5, fiber 0.1, carbs 1.3, protein 14.2

Garlic Zucchini Spread

Preparation time: 10 minutes
Cooking time: 15 minutes
Servings: 4

Ingredients:
- 4 zucchinis, roughly chopped
- 1 teaspoon garlic powder
- 1 tablespoon avocado oil
- ½ teaspoon salt

Directions:
1. Mix zucchini with garlic powder, avocado oil, and salt.
2. Put the mixture in the air fryer and bake at 375F for 15 minutes.
3. Then blend the cooked zucchini until you get smooth spread.

Nutrition: calories 38, fat 0.8, fiber 2.4, carbs 7.3, protein 2.5

Cream Cheese Rolls

Prep time: 15 minutes
Cooking time: 10 minutes
Servings: 4

Ingredients:
- 4 eggs, beaten
- ½ teaspoon coconut oil, melted
- ½ teaspoon chili flakes
- 2 tablespoons cream cheese

Directions:
1. Mix eggs with chili flakes.
2. Then brush the air fryer basket with coconut oil and preheat it to 395F.
3. Make 4 crepes from egg mixture and cook them in the air fryer basket.
4. Then spread the cream cheese over the every egg crepe and roll.

Nutrition: calories 85, fat 6.7, fiber 0, carbs 0.5, protein 5.9

Dill Omelet

Preparation time: 10 minutes
Cooking time: 15 minutes
Servings: 4

Ingredients:
- 8 eggs, beaten
- 1 tablespoon dill, dried
- ¼ cup of coconut milk
- ½ teaspoon coconut oil, melted

Directions:
1. Mix eggs with dill and coconut milk.
2. Brush the air fryer basket with coconut oil and pour the egg mixture inside.
3. Cook the omelet for 15 minutes at 385F.

Nutrition: calories 167, fat 12.9, fiber 0.4, carbs 2, protein 11.6

Soft Eggs

Prep time: 5 minutes
Cooking time: 16 minutes
Servings: 2

Ingredients:
- 6 eggs

Directions:
1. Put the eggs in the air fryer basket and cook them at 250F for 16 minutes.

Nutrition: calories 189, fat 13.1, fiber 0, carbs 1, protein 16.6

Greens Spread

Preparation time: 5 minutes
Cooking time: 10 minutes
Servings: 4

Ingredients:
- 2 tablespoons heavy cream
- 3 cups arugula, chopped
- 2 tablespoons dried oregano
- 1 oz pork rinds
- 1 oz Parmesan, grated

Directions:
1. Mix all ingredients in the air fryer basket and cook them at 365F for 10 minutes.
2. Then carefully mix the cooked mixture again and blend with the help of the immersion blender to get the spread texture.

Nutrition: calories 100, fat 7.2, fiber 1.2, carbs 2.5, protein 7.6

Cayenne Pepper Eggs

Prep time: 10 minutes
Cooking time: 12 minutes
Servings: 4

Ingredients:
- 1 teaspoon cayenne pepper
- 1 tablespoon butter, melted
- 8 eggs

Directions:
1. Preheat the air fryer to 395F.

2. Then brush the air fryer basket with butter and crack the eggs inside.
3. Sprinkle the eggs with cayenne pepper and cook them for 12 minutes.

Nutrition: calories 153, fat 11.7, fiber 0.1, carbs 0.9, protein 11.2

Swiss Chard Frittata

Preparation time: 5 minutes
Cooking time: 20 minutes
Servings: 4

Ingredients:
- 6 eggs, beaten
- 4 oz Swiss chard, chopped
- ¼ cup coconut cream
- 1 teaspoon coconut oil, melted
- ½ teaspoon ground turmeric
- ½ teaspoon salt

Directions:
1. In the mixing bowl mix all ingredients except coconut oil and make the small fritters.
2. Preheat the air fryer to 385F.
3. Brush it with coconut oil and put the fritters inside.
4. Cook them for 10 minutes per side.

Nutrition: calories 145, fat 11.4, fiber 0.9, carbs 2.6, protein 9.2

Mozzarella Sticks

Prep time: 15 minutes
Cooking time: 6 minutes
Servings: 6

Ingredients:
- 2 eggs, beaten
- 10 oz Mozzarella, cut into sticks
- 2 tablespoons coconut shred

Directions:

1. Dip Mozzarella sticks in the eggs and then coat in the coconut shred. Repeat the same step one more time.
2. After this, preheat the air fryer to 400F.
3. Put the sticks inside and roast them for 3 minutes per side.

Nutrition: calories 171, fat 11.5, fiber 0.3, carbs 2.5, protein 15.2

Egg and Spinach Muffins

Preparation time: 10 minutes
Cooking time: 15 minutes
Servings: 4

Ingredients:
- 1 cup Cheddar cheese, shredded
- 1 cup spinach, chopped
- 6 eggs, beaten
- 1 teaspoon coconut oil, melted
- 1 teaspoon dried oregano

Directions:
1. In the mixing bowl, mix Cheddar cheese with spinach, eggs, and dried oregano.
2. Brush the molds of the muffin with coconut oil and put the muffins mixture inside.
3. Bake the muffins at 385F for 15 minutes.

Nutrition: calories 221, fat 17.1, fiber 0.3, carbs 1.4, protein 15.6

Spinach Quesadilla

Prep time: 10 minutes
Cooking time: 3 minutes
Servings: 2

Ingredients:
- 2 keto tortillas
- ¼ cup Cheddar cheese, shredded
- ½ cup spinach, chopped
- 1 teaspoon avocado oil

Directions:
1. Brush the air fryer basket with avocado oil.
2. Then mix Cheddar cheese with spinach and put over the keto tortillas. Fold the tortillas and put in the air fryer basket.
3. Cook them at 400F for 3 minutes.

Nutrition: calories 212, fat 13, fiber 4.3, carbs 8.6, protein 15.8

Baked Bell Peppers Salad

Preparation time: 5 minutes
Cooking time: 10 minutes
Servings: 4

Ingredients:
- 1 cup bell pepper, chopped
- 1 teaspoon avocado oil
- 1 teaspoon olive oil
- 1 teaspoon dried cilantro
- ½ cup Mozzarella, shredded

Directions:
1. Mix bell pepper with avocado oil and put it in the air fryer.
2. Cook the vegetables for 10 minutes at 385F. Shake the bell peppers from time to time.
3. Then mix cooked bell peppers with olive oil, cilantro, and Mozzarella. Shake the cooked salad.

Nutrition: calories 31, fat 2, fiber 0.5, carbs 2.5, protein 1.3

Wrapped Bacon

Prep time: 15 minutes
Cooking time: 4 minutes
Servings: 2

Ingredients:
- 2 eggs, hard-boiled, peeled
- 4 bacon slices
- 1 teaspoon cream cheese
- 1 teaspoon ground black pepper
- 2 lettuce leaves

Directions:
1. Put the bacon slices in the air fryer and bake at 400F for 2 minutes per side.
2. Then wrap the eggs in the bacon and put on the lettuce leaves.
3. Add cream cheese and ground black pepper and fold the lettuce leaves.

Nutrition: calories 278, fat 20.9, fiber 0.3, carbs 1.8, protein 19.9

Kale Eggs

Preparation time: 10 minutes
Cooking time: 20 minutes
Servings: 4

Ingredients:
- 1 cup kale, chopped
- 6 eggs, beaten
- ¼ cup heavy cream
- ½ teaspoon ground black pepper
- ½ teaspoon coconut oil

Directions:
1. Grease ramekins with coconut oil.
2. Then mix kale with eggs and heavy cream. Add ground black pepper.
3. Pour the mixture in the ramekins and cook them in the air fryer basket at 375F for 20 minutes.

Nutrition: calories 134, fat 9.9, fiber 0.3, carbs 2.6, protein 9

Cinnamon Muffins

Prep time: 10 minutes
Cooking time: 10 minutes
Servings: 4

Ingredients:
- 1/3 cup coconut flour
- 2 tablespoons Erythritol
- ¼ teaspoon baking powder
- 1 teaspoon ground cinnamon
- 4 eggs, beaten
- 1 tablespoon coconut oil, softened

Directions:
1. Mix all ingredients in the mixing bowl.
2. Then transfer the mixture in the muffin molds and bake in the air fryer at 375F for 10 minutes.

Nutrition: calories 134, fat 8.8, fiber 4.3, carbs 7.6, protein 6.9

Jalapeno Bake

Preparation time: 5 minutes
Cooking time: 30 minutes
Servings: 6

Ingredients:
- 1 cup Mozzarella, shredded
- 2 jalapenos, sliced
- 6 eggs, beaten
- ¼ cup coconut cream
- 1 teaspoon coconut oil, softened
- ½ teaspoon ground black pepper

Directions:
1. Mix all ingredients in the baking pan and carefully stir until homogenous.
2. Then put the baking pan in the air fryer and cook the meal at 350F for 30 minutes.

Nutrition: calories 108, fat 8.4, fiber 0.4, carbs 1.5, protein 7.2

Zucchini Latkes

Prep time: 10 minutes
Cooking time: 8 minutes
Servings: 4

Ingredients:
- 2 zucchinis, grated
- 2 tablespoons coconut flour
- 1 teaspoon garlic powder
- 1 egg, beaten
- 2 oz swiss chard, chopped
- 1 teaspoon chili flakes
- 1 oz Parmesan, grated

Directions:
1.   In the mixing bowl, mix zucchinis with coconut flour, garlic powder, egg, swiss chard, chili flakes, and parmesan.
2.   Make the small latkes and put them in the preheated to 365F air fryer.
3.   Cook the latkes for 4 minutes per side.

Nutrition: calories 74, fat 3.2, fiber 2.9, carbs 7.2, protein 5.7

Parmesan Omelet

Preparation time: 5 minutes
Cooking time: 20 minutes
Servings: 4

Ingredients:
- 2 oz Parmesan, grated
- 5 eggs, beaten
- ½ teaspoon chili flakes
- ½ teaspoon dried parsley
- ¼ cup coconut cream
- ½ teaspoon coconut oil

Directions:
1.   Preheat the air fryer to 360F and grease the air fryer basket with coconut oil.
2.   Then mix eggs with Parmesan, chili flakes, dried parsley, and coconut cream.
3.   Pour the mixture in the air fryer and cook the omelet for 20 minutes.

Nutrition: calories 164, fat 12.7, fiber 0.3, carbs 1.8, protein 11.8

Bacon Cups

Prep time: 10 minutes
Cooking time: 14 minutes
Servings: 6

Ingredients:
- 6 eggs
- 6 bacon slices
- 1 teaspoon coconut oil
- 1 teaspoon pork rinds

Directions:
1.   Grease the ramekins with coconut oil and put the bacon slices inside.
2.   Cook the bacon in the air fryer at 365F for 2 minutes per side.
3.   Then crack the eggs over the bacon and sprinkle them with pork rinds.
4.   Bake the eggs for 10 minutes at 375F.

Nutrition: calories 186, fat 13.9, fiber 0, carbs 0.6, protein 14.1

Greens Salad

Preparation time: 15 minutes
Cooking time: 10 minutes
Servings: 4

Ingredients:

- 1 cup asparagus, chopped, cooked
- 6 oz Swiss chard, chopped
- 1 teaspoon garlic powder
- 1 tablespoon almonds, chopped
- 1 tablespoon apple cider vinegar
- 8 oz chicken fillet
- 1 teaspoon avocado oil
- 1 teaspoon olive oil

Directions:
1. Chop the chicken fillet roughly and mix it with olive oil, garlic powder, and apple cider vinegar.
2. Cook the chicken in the air fryer at 375F for 10 minutes.
3. Then mix cooked chicken with remaining ingredients and shake well.

Nutrition: calories 146, fat 6.4, fiber 1.7, carbs 3.8, protein 18.4

Sweet Buns

Prep time: 10 minutes
Cooking time: 12 minutes
Servings: 2

Ingredients:
- 2 tablespoons coconut flour
- ¼ teaspoon baking powder
- 1 teaspoon Erythritol
- 1 teaspoon mascarpone
- 1 teaspoon coconut oil, melted
- 2 eggs, beaten
- ¼ cup Mozzarella, shredded
- 1 teaspoon avocado oil

Directions:
1. Mix all ingredients in the mixing bowl and knead the dough.
2. Make the small buns and put them in the air fryer.
3. Bake the buns at 375F for 12 minutes or until they are light brown.

Nutrition: calories 131, fat 8.7, fiber 3.1, carbs 6, protein 7.9

Green Beans Salad

Preparation time: 10 minutes
Cooking time: 20 minutes
Servings: 4

Ingredients:
- 2 cups green beans, cut into medium pieces
- 2 cups fresh spinach, chopped
- 1 tablespoon avocado oil
- 1 tablespoons dried oregano
- 1 teaspoon coconut oil
- 1 teaspoon chili flakes

Directions:
1. Mix green beans with dried oregano, coconut oil, and chili flakes.
2. Cook the green beans in the air fryer basket for 20 minutes at 365F. Shake them from time to time.
3. Then mix cooked green beans with remaining ingredients and shake well.

Nutrition: calories 38, fat 1.8, fiber 2.8, carbs 5.4, protein 1.6

Meat Pizza

Prep time: 10 minutes
Cooking time: 15 minutes
Servings: 2

Ingredients:
- 8 oz ground beef
- 1 tablespoon marinara sauce
- ½ teaspoon dried oregano
- 1/3 cup Cheddar cheese, shredded
- ½ teaspoon coconut oil, melted
- ¼ teaspoon dried cilantro

Directions:

1. Mix ground beef with dried cilantro and dried oregano.
2. Brush the air fryer basket with coconut oil.
3. Make 2 flat balls from the ground beef and put them in the air fryer basket.
4. Top them with marinara sauce and Cheddar cheese.
5. Cook the pizza at 375F for 15 minutes.

Nutrition: calories 304, fat 14.7, fiber 0.4, carbs 1.6, protein 39.3

Nutmeg Omelet

Preparation time: 10 minutes
Cooking time: 20 minutes
Servings: 4

Ingredients:
- 6 eggs, beaten
- 1 teaspoon ground nutmeg
- 1 oz Parmesan
- ½ teaspoon coconut oil
- ¼ cup coconut cream

Directions:
1. Grate Parmesan and mix it with eggs, ground nutmeg, coconut cream, and coconut oil.
2. Pour the liquid in the air fryer basket and cook the omelet for 20 minutes at 355F.

Nutrition: calories 159, fat 12.4, fiber 0.4, carbs 1.9, protein 11

Mascarpone Omelet

Prep time: 8 minutes
Cooking time: 10 minutes
Servings: 6

Ingredients:

- 8 eggs, beaten
- ¼ cup mascarpone
- 1 teaspoon ground black pepper
- ½ teaspoon coconut oil

Directions:
1. Mix eggs with mascarpone and ground black pepper.
2. Then grease the air fryer basket with coconut oil.
3. Add the egg mixture and cook the omelet for 10 minutes at 385F.

Nutrition: calories 106, fat 7.6, fiber 0.1, carbs 1, protein 8.6

Chicken Bake

Preparation time: 5 minutes
Cooking time: 25 minutes
Servings: 4

Ingredients:
- 1 cup ground chicken
- ¼ cup Mozzarella, shredded
- 1 egg, beaten
- 1 teaspoon Italian seasonings
- 1 teaspoon coconut oil

Directions:
1. In the mixing bowl, mix all ingredients until you get a homogenous mixture.
2. Then put it in the air fryer basket and bake at 370F for 25 minutes.

Nutrition: calories 101, fat 5.5, fiber 0, carbs 0.3, protein 12

Keto Wrap

Prep time: 10 minutes
Cooking time: 15 minutes
Servings: 2

Ingredients:

- ½ cup ground pork
- 1 jalapeno pepper, chopped
- 1 teaspoon coconut oil
- 1 teaspoon plain yogurt
- ½ teaspoon dried oregano
- 4 lettuce leaves

Directions:
1. Mix the ground pork with jalapeno pepper and ground oregano.
2. Then preheat the air fryer to 365F.
3. Add coconut oil and ground pork mixture. Cook the mixture for 15 minutes. Stir it from time to time.
4. Then fill lettuce leaves with ground pork mixture. Add plain yogurt and wrap the lettuce leaves.

Nutrition: calories 141, fat 10.4, fiber 0.4, carbs 1.1, protein 10.3

Avocado Bake

Preparation time: 10 minutes
Cooking time: 20 minutes
Servings: 2

Ingredients:
- 1 avocado, pitted, halved
- 2 eggs
- 1 oz Parmesan, grated
- ½ teaspoon ground nutmeg

Directions:
1. Crack the eggs in the avocado hole and top them with Parmesan and ground nutmeg.
2. Then put the eggplants in the air fryer basket and cook at 375F for 20 minutes.

Nutrition: calories 316, fat 27.2, fiber 6.8, carbs 9.8, protein 12

Avocado Spread

Prep time: 10 minutes
Cooking time: 10 minutes
Servings: 4

Ingredients:
- 1 teaspoon garlic powder
- 1 avocado, pitted, peeled, chopped
- 1 tablespoon pork rinds, chopped
- 1 egg
- 1 tablespoon cream cheese

Directions:
1. Preheat the air fryer to 375F.
2. Mix beaten egg with pork rinds and pour the mixture in the air fryer.
3. Cook it at 385F for 10 minutes. Stir the cooked egg mixture well.
4. Then mix it with garlic powder, avocado, and cream cheese. Blend the mixture well.

Nutrition: calories 149, fat 13, fiber 3.4, carbs 5, protein 4.9

Kale Mix

Preparation time: 5 minutes
Cooking time: 20 minutes
Servings: 4

Ingredients:
- 4 kalamata olives, chopped
- 1 cup kale, chopped
- 2 oz Provolone cheese, grated
- 4 eggs, beaten
- ½ teaspoon smoked paprika

Directions:
1. Mix all ingredients in the mixing bowl.
2. Then pour it in the air fryer basket.
3. Flatten the mixture and cook it at 360F for 20 minutes.

Nutrition: calories 127, fat 8.6, fiber 0.5, carbs 2.8, protein 9.7

Mozzarella Balls

Prep time: 15 minutes
Cooking time: 12 minutes
Servings: 6

Ingredients:
- 4 tablespoons coconut flour
- ½ cup Mozzarella cheese, shredded
- 1 teaspoon Erythritol
- 2 tablespoons coconut oil, softened
- ¼ teaspoon baking powder
- 1 egg, beaten

Directions:
1. In the mixing bowl, mix coconut flour with Mozzarella cheese, Erythritol, coconut oil, baking powder, and egg. Knead the dough.
2. Make the balls and put them in the air fryer.
3. Cook the balls at 365F for 12 minutes.

Nutrition: calories 76, fat 6.2, fiber 2, carbs 3.6, protein 2.3

Swiss Chard Bake

Preparation time: 10 minutes
Cooking time: 15 minutes
Servings: 4

Ingredients:
- 4 eggs, beaten
- 1 tablespoon coconut cream
- 2 oz Swiss Chard, chopped
- ½ teaspoon coconut oil
- 1 oz Provolone cheese, grated

Directions:
1. Grease the air fryer basket with coconut oil.
2. Then pour eggs inside.

3. Add coconut cream, Provolone cheese, and Swiss Chard.
4. Cook the meal at 375F for 16 minutes or until the eggs are firm.

Nutrition: calories 104, fat 7.8, fiber 0.3, carbs 1.2, protein 7.7

Tender Muffins

Prep time: 15 minutes
Cooking time: 12 minutes
Servings: 4

Ingredients:
- 4 slices of ham, chopped
- 4 eggs, beaten
- ¼ cup coconut cream
- 1 teaspoon dried dill
- 1 teaspoon coconut oil, softened
- ½ teaspoon chives, chopped

Directions:
1. In the mixing bowl, mix ham with eggs, coconut cream, dried dill, coconut oil, and chives.
2. Put the mixture in the muffin molds and bale at 365F for 12 minutes.

Nutrition: calories 153, fat 11.5, fiber 0.7, carbs 2.4, protein 10.6

Fish Eggs

Preparation time: 5 minutes
Cooking time: 20 minutes
Servings: 4

Ingredients:
- 1 teaspoon chives, chopped
- 5 oz cod fillet, chopped, boiled
- 4 eggs, beaten
- ½ teaspoon ground coriander
- ½ teaspoon coconut oil, melted
- ½ teaspoon salt

Directions:
1. Shred the cod fillet and mix it with chives, eggs, ground coriander, and salt.
2. Brush the air fryer basket with coconut oil and pour the egg mixture inside.
3. Bake the fish eggs at 360F for 20 minutes.

Nutrition: calories 96, fat 5.3, fiber 0, carbs 0.4, protein 11.9

Chilies Casserole

Prep time: 10 minutes
Cooking time: 15 minutes
Servings: 2

Ingredients:
- 1 chili pepper, chopped
- 1 cup ground chicken
- ¼ cup Mozzarella, shredded
- ½ teaspoon ground cinnamon
- ½ teaspoon coconut oil
- ¼ cup cauliflower, chopped

Directions:
1. Mix chili pepper with ground chicken, Mozzarella, ground cinnamon, and cauliflower.
2. Brush the air fryer basket with coconut oil and put the mixture inside.
3. Bake the casserole at 375F for 15 minutes.

Nutrition: calories 158 fat 7, fiber 0.7, carbs 1.4, protein 21.6

Sides and Snacks

Turmeric Cauliflower Rice

Preparation time: 5 minutes
Cooking time: 20 minutes
Servings: 4

Ingredients:
- 3 cups cauliflower, shredded
- 1 tablespoon coconut oil
- 1 teaspoon ground turmeric
- ½ teaspoon dried oregano

Directions:
1. Grease the air fryer basket with coconut oil.
2. Then mix cauliflower with ground turmeric and dried oregano. Put the mixture in the air fryer.
3. Cook the cauliflower rice at 360F for 20 minutes. Shake the rice from time to time to avoid burning.

Nutrition: calories 51, fat 3.6, fiber 2.1, carbs 4.5, protein 1.6

Portobello Patties

Prep time: 10 minutes
Cooking time: 8 minutes
Servings: 4

Ingredients:
- 10 oz Portobello mushrooms, diced
- 1 egg, beaten
- 3 oz Monterey Jack cheese, shredded
- 1 teaspoon dried cilantro
- ½ teaspoon white pepper
- 1 teaspoon avocado oil
- 2 tablespoons coconut flour

Directions:

1. Mix mushrooms with egg, Monterey Jack cheese, cilantro, white pepper, and coconut flour.
2. Make the patties from the mushroom mixture.
3. Then brush the air fryer basket with avocado oil and put the patties inside.
4. Cook them at 375F for 4 minutes per side.

Nutrition: calories 145, fat 8.6, fiber 3.7, carbs 7.6, protein 10.5

Cauliflower Bake

Preparation time: 15 minutes
Cooking time: 20 minutes
Servings: 2

Ingredients:
- 1 cup cauliflower, chopped
- 2 eggs, beaten
- ½ cup Cheddar cheese, shredded
- ½ teaspoon chili powder
- 1 teaspoon coconut oil
- ½ cup heavy cream

Directions:
1. Grease the baking pan with coconut oil.
2. After this, mix cauliflower with eggs, Cheddar cheese, chili powder, and heavy cream.
3. Transfer the mixture in the prepared baking pan and flatten gently.
4. Put the baking pan in the air fryer basket and cook the meal at 385F for 20 minutes.

Nutrition: calories 314, fat 27.3, fiber 1.5, carbs 4.6, protein 14.3

Cilantro Tofu

Prep time: 15 minutes
Cooking time: 8 minutes
Servings: 2

Ingredients:
- 10 oz tofu, cubed
- 1 teaspoon avocado oil
- 1 teaspoon dried cilantro
- ½ teaspoon ground paprika
- ½ teaspoon ground black pepper
- 1 tablespoon apple cider vinegar

Directions:
1. Mix avocado oil with dried cilantro, ground paprika, ground black pepper, and apple cider vinegar.
2. Then mix cubed tofu with avocado oil mixture and leave for 10 minutes to marinate.
3. Meanwhile, preheat the air fryer to 385F.
4. Put the tofu cubes in the air fryer in one layer and roast for 4 minutes per side.

Nutrition: calories 107, fat 6.3, fiber 1.7, carbs 3.3, protein 11.8

Garlic Brussels Sprouts

Preparation time: 10 minutes
Cooking time: 20 minutes
Servings: 4

Ingredients:
- 1 pound Brussels sprouts, trimmed and halved
- 1 tablespoon garlic powder
- 1 tablespoon coconut oil
- ½ teaspoon ground black pepper

Directions:

1. Mix Brussel sprouts with garlic powder, coconut oil, and ground black pepper.
2. Then put the vegetables in the air fryer basket and cook at 375F for 20 minutes. Shake the vegetables from time to time to avoid burning.

Nutrition: calories 86, fat 3.8, fiber 4.5, carbs 12, protein 4.3

Zucchini Balls

Prep time: 15 minutes
Cooking time: 6 minutes
Servings: 4

Ingredients:
- 1 zucchini, grated
- ½ cup Cheddar cheese, shredded
- 1 egg, beaten
- 1 teaspoon chili powder
- 1 teaspoon avocado oil

Directions:
1. In the mixing bowl mix zucchini with cheese, egg, and chili powder.
2. Make the balls from the zucchini mixture and put it in the air fryer.
3. Sprinkle the zucchini balls with avocado oil and cook at 385F for 6 minutes or until the zucchini balls are light brown.

Nutrition: calories 84, fat 6.1, fiber 0.8, carbs 2.3, protein 5.6

Mustard Vegetables

Preparation time: 10 minutes
Cooking time: 20 minutes
Servings: 4

Ingredients:
- 1 cup cauliflower, chopped
- 1 cup broccoli, chopped

- 1 tablespoon mustard
- 1 tablespoon avocado oil
- 1 teaspoon chili powder
- ½ teaspoon dried dill
- 1 teaspoon apple cider vinegar

Directions:
1. In the shallow bowl mix mustard with avocado oil, chili powder, dried dill, and apple cider vinegar.
2. Then put cauliflower and broccoli in the air fryer. Sprinkle the vegetables with mustard mixture and close the lid.
3. Cook the vegetables at 385F for 20 minutes. Shake the vegetables after 10 minutes of cooking.

Nutrition: calories 34, fat 1.5, fiber 2, carbs 4.5, protein 2

Mushroom Fritters

Prep time: 10 minutes
Cooking time: 6 minutes
Servings: 2

Ingredients:
- 1 cup mushrooms, grinded
- 1 teaspoon garlic powder
- 1 egg, beaten
- 3 teaspoons coconut flour
- ½ teaspoon chili powder
- 1 teaspoon coconut oil
- 1 tablespoon almond flour

Directions:
1. In the mixing bowl, mix mushrooms with garlic powder, egg, coconut flour, chili powder, and almond flour.
2. Make the mushroom fritters and put them in the air fryer basket.
3. Add coconut oil and cook the fritters at 400F for 3 minutes per side.

Nutrition: calories 139, fat 8.2, fiber 5.6, carbs 10.2, protein 7.2

Keto Risotto

Preparation time: 5 minutes
Cooking time: 20 minutes
Servings: 4

Ingredients:
- 1 pound mushrooms, diced
- ¼ cup Cheddar cheese, shredded
- 3 cups cauliflower, shredded
- 1 cup beef broth
- 1 teaspoon dried oregano
- 1 teaspoon dried cilantro
- 1 tablespoon coconut oil

Directions:
1. Mix all ingredients in the air fryer basket and cook at 375F for 20 minutes.
2. Stir the risotto every 5 minutes to avoid burning.

Nutrition: calories 112, fat 6.5, fiber 3.2, carbs 8.3, protein 8.1

Broccoli Tots

Prep time: 15 minutes
Cooking time: 8 minutes
Servings: 4

Ingredients:
- 1 teaspoon mascarpone
- 5 oz Cheddar cheese, shredded
- 3 cups broccoli, chopped, boiled
- ¼ teaspoon onion powder
- 1 teaspoon avocado oil

Directions:
1. In the mixing bowl mix mascarpone with Cheddar cheese, broccoli, and onion powder.

2. Make the broccoli tots from the mixture and put them in the air fryer basket in one layer.
3. Sprinkle the broccoli tots with avocado oil and cook them at 400F for 8 minutes.

Nutrition: calories 166, fat 12.1, fiber 1.9, carbs 4.7, protein 10.5

Chives and Spinach

Preparation time: 5 minutes
Cooking time: 10 minutes
Servings: 4

Ingredients:
- 3 cups spinach, chopped
- 1 oz chives, chopped
- ½ cup heavy cream
- 1 teaspoon chili powder

Directions:
1. Mix spinach with chives, heavy cream, and chili powder.
2. Put the mixture in the air fryer basket and cook at 360F for 10 minutes.
3. Carefully mix the meal before serving.

Nutrition: calories 61, fat 5.8, fiber 0.9, carbs 1.9, protein 1.3

Chili Zucchini Tots

Prep time: 10 minutes
Cooking time: 12 minutes
Servings: 4

Ingredients:
- 3 zucchinis, grated
- ½ cup coconut flour
- 2 eggs, beaten
- 1 teaspoon chili flakes
- 1 teaspoon salt

- 1 teaspoon avocado oil

Directions:
In the bowl mix up grated carrot, salt, ground cumin, zucchini, Provolone cheese, chili flakes, egg, and coconut flour. Stir the mass with the help of the spoon and make the small balls. Then line the air fryer basket with baking paper and sprinkle it with sunflower oil. Put the zucchini balls in the air fryer basket and cook them for 12 minutes at 375F. Shake the balls every 2 minutes to avoid burning.

Nutrition: calories 122, fat 7.4, fiber 3.7, carbs 7.3, protein 7.2

Broccoli Hash Brown

Preparation time: 5 minutes
Cooking time: 15 minutes
Servings: 4

Ingredients:
- 2 cups broccoli, chopped
- 3 eggs, whisked
- 1 tablespoon coconut oil
- 1 teaspoon dried oregano

Directions:
1. Mix broccoli with eggs and put the mixture in the air fryer.
2. Add coconut oil and dried oregano.
3. Cook the meal at 400F for 15 minutes. Stir the meal every 5 minutes.

Nutrition: calories 93, fat 6.9, fiber 1.3, carbs 3.5, protein 5.5

Parm Bites

Prep time: 10 minutes
Cooking time: 10 minutes
Servings: 5

Ingredients:
- 2 medium eggplants, trimmed, sliced
- 4 oz Parmesan, grated
- 1 teaspoon coconut oil, melted

Directions:
1. Grease the air fryer basket with coconut oil.
2. Then put the sliced eggplants in the air fryer basket in one layer.
3. Top them with Parmesan and cook the meal at 390F for 10 minutes.

Nutrition: calories 136, fat 6.2, fiber 7.7, carbs 13.7, protein 9.4

Broccoli Puree

Preparation time: 10 minutes
Cooking time: 20 minutes
Servings: 4

Ingredients:
- 1-pound broccoli, chopped
- 1 tablespoon coconut oil
- ¼ cup heavy cream
- 1 teaspoon salt

Directions:
1. Put coconut oil in the air fryer.
2. Add broccoli, heavy cream, and salt.
3. Cook the mixture for 20 minutes at 365F.
4. Then mash the cooked broccoli mixture until you get the soft puree.

Nutrition: calories 94, fat 6.6, fiber 3, carbs 7.7, protein 3.3

Garlic Brussel Sprouts

Prep time: 10 minutes
Cooking time: 13 minutes
Servings: 6

Ingredients:
- 1-pound Brussel sprouts
- 1 teaspoon garlic powder
- 1 teaspoon ground coriander
- 1 tablespoon coconut oil
- 1 tablespoon apple cider vinegar

Directions:
1. Put coconut oil in the air fryer.
2. Then add Brussel sprouts, garlic powder, ground coriander, and apple cider vinegar.
3. Shake the vegetables gently and cook at 390F for 13 minutes. Shake the Brussel sprouts from time to time to avoid burning.

Nutrition: calories 54, fat 2.5, fiber 2.9, carbs 7.2, protein 2.7

Coriander Fennel

Preparation time: 5 minutes
Cooking time: 15 minutes
Servings: 4

Ingredients:
- 1 pound fennel bulb, cut into small wedges
- 1 teaspoon ground coriander
- 1 tablespoon avocado oil
- ½ teaspoon salt

Directions:
1. Rub the fennel bulb with ground coriander, avocado oil, and salt.
2. Put it in the air fryer basket and cook at 390F for 15 minutes. Flip the fennel on another side after 7 minutes of cooking.

Nutrition: calories 40, fat 0.7, fiber 3.7, carbs 8.5, protein 1.2

Turmeric Tempeh

Prep time: 8 minutes
Cooking time: 12 minute
Servings: 4

Ingredients:
- 1 teaspoon apple cider vinegar
- 1 tablespoon avocado oil
- ¼ teaspoon ground turmeric
- 6 oz tempeh, chopped

Directions:
1. Mix avocado oil with apple cider vinegar and ground turmeric.
2. Then sprinkle the tempeh with turmeric mixture and put it in the air fryer basket.
3. Cook the tempeh at 350F for 12 minutes. Shake it after 6 minutes of cooking.

Nutrition: calories 87, fat 5, fiber 0.2, carbs 4.3, protein 7.9

Banana Peppers Mix

Preparation time: 10 minutes
Cooking time: 20 minutes
Servings: 4

Ingredients:
- 8 oz banana peppers, chopped
- 1 tablespoon avocado oil
- 1 tablespoon dried oregano
- 2 tablespoons mascarpone
- 1 cup Monterey Jack cheese, shredded

Directions:
1. Brush the baking pan with avocado oil.
2. After this, mix banana peppers with dried oregano and mascarpone and put in the prepared baking pan.

3. Top the peppers with Monterey Jack cheese and place in the air fryer basket.
4. Cook the meal at 365F for 20 minutes.

Nutrition: calories 133, fat 10.1, fiber 1.1, carbs 2.9, protein 8.2

Keto "Potato"

Prep time: 10 minutes
Cooking time: 20 minutes
Servings: 2

Ingredients:
- 2 cups cauliflower, chopped
- 1 oz Parmesan, grated
- 1 tablespoon avocado oil

Directions:
1. Sprinkle the cauliflower with avocado oil and put it in the air fryer.
2. Cook it at 390F for 10 minutes.
3. Then shake the cauliflower and sprinkle with Parmesan.
4. Cook the meal at 390F for 10 minutes more.

Nutrition: calories 80, fat 4, fiber 2.8, carbs 6.2, protein 6.6

Keto Coleslaw

Preparation time: 10 minutes
Cooking time: 20 minutes
Servings: 4

Ingredients:
- 1 cup white cabbage, shredded
- 2 tablespoons apple cider vinegar
- ½ cup heavy cream
- 1 teaspoon ground black pepper
- 1 tablespoon Dijon mustard

Directions:

1. Mix white cabbage with heavy cream and put it in the air fryer basket.
2. Cook the cabbage for 20 minutes at 350F. Stir it from time to time.
3. Then transfer the white cabbage mixture in the salad bowl.
4. Add all remaining ingredients and carefully mix.

Nutrition: calories 62, fat 5.8, fiber 0.7, carbs 2.1, protein 0.8

Coconut Brussel Sprouts

Prep time: 10 minutes
Cooking time: 15 minutes
Servings: 4

Ingredients:
• 8 oz Brussels sprouts
• 1 tablespoon coconut shred
• 1 tablespoon coconut oil
• 1 teaspoon ground paprika
• 1 teaspoon ground black pepper

Directions:
1. Put all ingredients in the air fryer basket and shake well.
2. Cook the meal at 380F for 15 minutes. Shake the meal while cooking every 5 minutes.

Nutrition: calories 64, fat 4.2, fiber 2.5, carbs 6.5, protein 2.1

Cabbage Steaks

Preparation time: 10 minutes
Cooking time: 25 minutes
Servings: 4

Ingredients:
• 1-pound white cabbage, cut into steaks
• 1 tablespoon avocado oil

• 1 teaspoon salt
• 1 teaspoon apple cider vinegar
• ½ teaspoon mustard

Directions:
1. Rub the white cabbage steaks with avocado oil, salt, apple cider vinegar, and mustard.
2. Then put them in the air fryer basket in one layer and cook at 375F for 15 minutes.
3. After this, flip the cabbage steaks on another side and cook them for 10 minutes more.

Nutrition: calories 35, fat 0.7, fiber 3.1, carbs 6.9, protein 1.6

Green BLT

Prep time: 10 minutes
Cooking time: 4 minutes
Servings: 4

Ingredients:
• 2 tomatillos
• ¼ cup almond flour
• 2 eggs, beaten
• ¼ teaspoon ground black pepper
• ¼ teaspoon chili powder
• 1 oz Monterey Jack cheese, shredded
• 4 lettuce leaves

Directions:
1. Slice the tomatillos into 4 slices and sprinkle with ground black pepper and chili powder.
2. Dip the tomatillos in the eggs and coat in the almond flour. Repeat this step one more time.
3. After this, put the tomatillos in the air fryer basket and cook them at 400F for 2 minutes per side.
4. Then put the cooked tomatillos on the lettuce leaves and top with Monterey Jack cheese.

Nutrition: calories 107, fat 7.9, fiber 1.2, carbs 3, protein 6.2

Rutabaga Bites

Preparation time: 10 minutes
Cooking time: 20 minutes
Servings: 4

Ingredients:
* 15 ounces rutabaga, cut into fries
* 4 tablespoons avocado oil
* 1 teaspoon garlic powder

Directions:
1. Mix rutabaga with garlic powder and avocado oil and put it in the air fryer.
2. Cook the rutabaga bites at 360F for 20 minutes. Shake them from time to time to avoid burning.

Nutrition: calories 59, fat 2, fiber 3.3, carbs 9.9, protein 1.6

Keto Mac&Cheese

Prep time: 10 minutes
Cooking time: 10 minutes
Servings: 4

Ingredients:
* 2 cups cauliflower, chopped
* 1 teaspoon avocado oil
* 1 teaspoon salt
* 1 teaspoon dried oregano
* ½ cup Monterey Jack, shredded
* ½ cup of heavy cream
* ½ teaspoon coconut oil

Directions:
1. Put the cauliflower in the air fryer basket.

2. Sprinkle it with avocado oil, salt, dried oregano, heavy cream, and coconut oil.
3. Then shake the mixture and top it with Monterey Jack cheese.
4. Cook the meal at 400F for 10 minutes.

Nutrition: calories 127, fat 10.9, fiber 1.5, carbs 3.9, protein 4.9

Eggplant Mash

Preparation time: 10 minutes
Cooking time: 15 minutes
Servings: 4

Ingredients:
* ½ cup Mozzarella, shredded
* 2 eggplants, trimmed
* 1 tablespoon avocado oil
* ½ teaspoon dried cilantro

Directions:
1. Chop the eggplants and sprinkle them with avocado oil.
2. Cook the vegetables in the air fryer for 15 minutes.
3. Then transfer them in the blender. Add cilantro and cheese.
4. Blend the mixture until smooth.

Nutrition: calories 83, fat 1.6, fiber 9.8, carbs 16.4, protein 3.7

Cheesy Asparagus

Prep time: 10 minutes
Cooking time: 5 minutes
Servings: 3

Ingredients:
* 9 oz Asparagus
* 1 oz Parmesan, grated
* 1 teaspoon avocado oil

Directions:
1. Chop the asparagus roughly and sprinkle with avocado oil.
2. Put it in the air fryer basket and cook at 400F for 5 minutes.
3. Then transfer the cooked asparagus in the serving plate and sprinkle with Parmesan.

Nutrition: calories 49, fat 2.3, fiber 1.9, carbs 3.7, protein 4.9

Vegetable Roast

Preparation time: 5 minutes
Cooking time: 20 minutes
Servings: 4

Ingredients:
- 1 cup cauliflower, chopped
- 6 oz asparagus, chopped
- 1 tablespoon coconut oil
- 1 teaspoon Italian seasonings
- 1 teaspoon salt

Directions:
1. Put all ingredients in the air fryer basket and shake well.
2. Cook the vegetables at 380F for 20 minutes. Stir them after 10 minutes of cooking.

Nutrition: calories 48, fat 3.8, fiber 1.5, carbs 3.1, protein 1.4

Bacon and Spinach Bowl

Prep time: 10 minutes
Cooking time: 6 minutes
Servings: 2

Ingredients:
- 2 cups spinach, chopped
- 1 oz bacon, chopped
- 1 pecan, chopped
- 1 teaspoon ground black pepper

- 2 oz Mozzarella, shredded

Directions:
1. Put the bacon in the air fryer basket and cook at 400f for 6 minutes.
2. Then mix the cooked bacon with remaining ingredients.

Nutrition: calories 215, fat 16.1, fiber 1.7, carbs 4, protein 15

Chicken Bites

Preparation time: 10 minutes
Cooking time: 20 minutes
Servings: 4

Ingredients:
- 1 teaspoon onion powder
- 1-pound chicken breast, skinless, boneless, chopped
- 1 teaspoon chili powder
- 1 teaspoon coconut oil

Directions:
1. Mix chicken breast with onion powder, chili powder, and coconut oil.
2. Put the chicken in the air fryer in one layer and cook at 380F for 10 minutes per side.

Nutrition: calories 143, fat 4.1, fiber 0.3, carbs 0.8, protein 24.2

Mozzarella Turnovers

Prep time: 15 minutes
Cooking time: 3 minutes
Servings: 10

Ingredients:
- 10 Mozzarella cheese slices
- 4 zucchinis, sliced

Directions:

1. Put the Mozzarella slices on the zucchini slices and fold them. Secure the turnovers with a toothpick if needed.
2. Cook the meal at 400F in the air fryer for 3 minutes.

Nutrition: calories 93, fat 5.1, fiber 0.9, carbs 3.6, protein 9

Kale Chips

Preparation time: 5 minutes
Cooking time: 30 minutes
Servings: 8

Ingredients:
- 2 oz Parmesan, grated
- 12 oz kale, roughly chopped

Directions:
1. Mix kale with Parmesan and put in the air fryer.
2. Cook the chips at 350F for 10 minutes.
3. Then shake them and cook for 20 minutes more.

Nutrition: calories 44, fat 1.5, fiber 0.6, carbs 4.7, protein 3.6

Portobello Pizza

Prep time: 10 minutes
Cooking time: 7 minutes
Servings:6

Ingredients:
- 6 Portobello mushroom caps
- 1 tomato, chopped
- 1 cup Mozzarella, shredded
- 1 teaspoon dried basil
- 1 teaspoon coconut oil

Directions:

1. Grease the air fryer basket with coconut oil and put the Portobello mushroom cups inside.
2. Top them with tomato, dried basil, and Mozzarella.
3. Close the lid and cook pizza at 400F for 7 minutes.

Nutrition: calories 29, fat 1.7, fiber 0.5, carbs 2, protein 2.1

Parmesan Chips

Preparation time: 2 minutes
Cooking time: 5 minutes
Servings: 4

Ingredients:
- 6 oz Parmesan, grated

Directions:
1. Make the small circles from the grated cheese in the air fryer basket and cook them at 400F for 5 minutes.
2. Then cool the Parmesan chips and put them on the plate.

Nutrition: calories 137, fat 9.1, fiber 0, carbs 1.5, protein 13.7

Vegetable Crackers
Prep time: 15 minutes
Cooking time: 12 minutes
Servings:8

Ingredients:
- 1 cup zucchini, grated
- 2 tablespoons flax meal
- 2 tablespoons coconut flour
- 1 teaspoon coconut oil
- 1 egg, beaten

Directions:
1. Mix zucchini with flax meal, coconut flour, and egg.

2. Roll the dough and make the crackers with the help of the cutter.
3. Grease the air fryer basket with coconut oil and put the crackers inside.
4. Bake them at 400F for 6 minutes per side or until they are golden brown.

Nutrition: calories 30, fat 2, fiber 1.4, carbs 2.3, protein 1.5

Olives Cakes

Preparation time: 10 minutes
Cooking time: 12 minutes
Servings: 6

Ingredients:
- 2 tablespoons fresh cilantro, chopped
- 1 egg, beaten
- ½ cup coconut flour
- 1 oz scallions, chopped
- 6 oz kalamata olives, pitted and minced

Directions:
1. Mix fresh cilantro with egg, coconut flour, scallions, and olives.
2. Make the small cakes and put them in the air fryer on one layer.
3. Cook the cakes at 385F for 6 minutes per side.

Nutrition: calories 85, fat 4.8, fiber 5, carbs 8.9, protein 2.6

Pork Minis

Prep time: 10 minutes
Cooking time: 15 minutes
Servings: 4

Ingredients:
- 1 cup ground pork
- 1 teaspoon Italian seasonings
- ¼ cup Cheddar cheese, shredded
- 1 teaspoon tomato paste
- ½ teaspoon coconut oil

Directions:
1. In the mixing bowl, mix ground pork with Italian seasonings, Cheddar cheese, and tomato paste.
2. Then make the minis from the mixture.
3. Grease the air fryer basket with coconut oil and put the pork minis inside.
4. Cook them for 15 minutes at 375F.

Nutrition: calories 157, fat 6.2, fiber 0.1, carbs 0.5, protein 23.6

Rosemary Balls

Preparation time: 5 minutes
Cooking time: 12 minutes
Servings: 6

Ingredients:
- ¼ teaspoon ground black pepper
- 1 ½ cup almond flour
- 1 teaspoon garlic powder
- 1 teaspoon dried rosemary
- 2 eggs, beaten
- 1 cup mushrooms, diced

Directions:
1. In the mixing bowl, mix almond flour with garlic powder, dried rosemary, eggs, and mushrooms.
2. Make the balls and put them in the air fryer.
3. Cook the meal at 360F for 12 minutes.

Nutrition: calories 68, fat 4.9, fiber 1, carbs 2.5, protein 3.8

Keto Chaffle

Prep time: 10 minutes
Cooking time: 8 minutes
Servings: 4

Ingredients:
• 4 eggs, beaten
• 2 oz pancetta, chopped, cooked
• 2 oz Provolone cheese, grated
• ¼ teaspoon salt
• 1 teaspoon avocado oil

Directions:
1. Brush the air fryer basket with avocado oil.
2. Then mix pancetta with Provolone cheese and salt.
3. Pout the liquid in the air fryer basket and cook it at 400F for 8 minutes.

Nutrition: calories 191, fat 14.2, fiber 0.1, carbs 0.9, protein 14.4

Classic Zucchini Chips

Preparation time: 5 minutes
Cooking time: 35 minutes
Servings: 6

Ingredients:
• 3 zucchinis, thinly sliced
• 1 teaspoon salt

Directions:
1. Put the zucchini in the air fryer and sprinkle with salt.
2. Cook them at 350F for 35 minutes. Shake the zucchini every 5 minutes.

Nutrition: calories 16, fat 0.2, fiber 1.1, carbs 3.3, protein 1.2

Seaweed Crisps

Prep time: 10 minutes
Cooking time: 5 minutes

Servings: 4

Ingredients:
• 3 nori sheets
• 1 teaspoon nutritional yeast
• 2 tablespoons water

Directions:
1. Cut the nori sheets roughly and put in the air fryer basket.
2. Sprinkle the nori sheets with water and nutritional yeast and cook at 375F for 5 minutes.

Nutrition: calories 4, fat 0.1, fiber 0.2, carbs 0.6, protein 0.8

Avocado Sticks

Preparation time: 10 minutes
Cooking time: 14 minutes
Servings: 4

Ingredients:
• 1 avocado, pitted, halves
• 1 egg, beaten
• 1 tablespoon coconut shred

Directions:
1. Cut the avocado halves into 4 wedges and dip in the egg.
2. Then coat the avocado in coconut shred and put in the air fryer.
3. Cook the avocado sticks at 375F for 7 minutes per side.

Nutrition: calories 131, fat 12.1, fiber 3.6, carbs 4.9, protein 2.3

Mozzarella Sticks

Prep time: 10 minutes
Cooking time: 4 minutes
Servings: 4

Ingredients:

- 1 egg, beaten
- 4 tablespoons almond flour
- 9 oz Mozzarella, cut into sticks

Directions:
1.   Dip the mozzarella sticks in the egg and them coat in the almond flour.
2.   Then put the mozzarella sticks in the air fryer basket and cook at 400F for 4 minutes.

Nutrition: calories 238, fat 15.7, fiber 0.8, carbs 3.8, protein 20.9

Lettuce Wraps

Preparation time: 10 minutes
Cooking time: 4 minutes
Servings: 12

Ingredients:
- 12 bacon strips
- 12 lettuce leaves
- 1 tablespoon mustard
- 1 tablespoon apple cider vinegar

Directions:
1.   Put the bacon in the air fryer in one layer and cook at 400f for 2 minutes per side.
2.   Then sprinkle the bacon with mustard and apple cider vinegar and put on the lettuce.
3.   Wrap the lettuce into rolls.

Nutrition: calories 105, fat 9.3, fiber 0.2, carbs 0.5, protein 4.3

Carrot Chips

Prep time: 10 minutes
Cooking time: 13 minute
Servings:8

Ingredients:
- 3 carrots, thinly sliced

- 1 teaspoon avocado oil

Directions:
1.   Put the carrots in the air fryer basket, sprinkle with avocado oil.
2.   Cook the carrot chips for 30 minutes at 355F. Shake the carrot chips every 5 minutes.

Nutrition: calories 10, fat 0.1, fiber 0.6, carbs 2.3, protein 0.2

Crunchy Bacon
Preparation time: 5 minutes
Cooking time: 8 minutes
Servings: 4

Ingredients:
- 8 bacon slices
- 1 teaspoon Erythritol

Directions:
1.   Sprinkle the bacon with Erythritol and put in the air fryer basket in one layer.
2.   Cook it for 4 minutes per side or until the bacon is crunchy.

Nutrition: calories 206, fat 15.9, fiber 0, carbs 1.8, protein 14.1

Keto Granola

Prep time: 10 minutes
Cooking time: 12 minutes
Servings:4

Ingredients:
- 1 teaspoon monk fruit
- 2 teaspoons coconut oil
- 3 pecans, chopped
- 1 teaspoon pumpkin pie spices
- 1 tablespoon coconut shred
- 3 oz almonds, chopped
- 1 tablespoon flax seeds

Directions:
1. In the mixing bowl, mix all ingredients from the list above.
2. Make the small balls from the mixture and put them in the air fryer.
3. Cook the granola for 6 minutes per side at 365F.
4. Cool the cooked granola.

Nutrition: calories 239, fat 22.3, fiber 4.6, carbs 7.4, protein 6

Bacon Pickles

Preparation time: 5 minutes
Cooking time: 6 minutes
Servings: 4

Ingredients:
*   4 pickled cucumbers
*   4 bacon slices

Directions:
1. Preheat the air fryer to 400F and put the bacon inside.
2. Cook it for 3 minutes per side.
3. Then cool the bacon and wrap pickled cucumbers in the bacon.

Nutrition: calories 148, fat 8.3, fiber 1.5, carbs 11.2, protein 9

Smokies

Prep time: 10 minutes
Cooking time: 10 minutes
Servings: 10

Ingredients:
* 12 oz pork smokies
* 1 teaspoon cayenne pepper
* 1 tablespoon coconut oil
* 1 teaspoon keto tomato paste

Directions:

1. Mix pork smokies with cayenne pepper, coconut oil, and tomato paste.
2. Put them in the air fryer basket and cook for 5 minutes per side at 375F.

Nutrition: calories 115, fat 10.6, fiber 0.1, carbs 0.8, protein 4.3

Avocado and Pork Rinds Balls

Preparation time: 10 minutes
Cooking time: 5 minutes
Servings: 4

Ingredients:
*   1 avocado, peeled, pitted and mashed
*   1 tablespoon cream cheese
*   2 oz pork rinds
*   1 teaspoon dried oregano

Directions:
1. Preheat the air fryer to 360F and put the pork rinds inside. Cook them for 5 minutes.
2. Then mix the pork rinds with dried oregano, cream cheese, and mashed avocado.
3. Make the balls from the mixture.

Nutrition: calories 193, fat 15.8, fiber 3.5, carbs 4.6, protein 10.3

Chicken Skin

Prep time: 10 minutes
Cooking time: 10 minutes
Servings: 3

Ingredients:
* 6 oz chicken skin
* 1 teaspoon avocado oil
* ½ teaspoon ground black pepper

Directions:

1. Chop the chicken skin roughly and mix it with avocado oil and ground black pepper.
2. Put the chicken skin in the air fryer basket and cook at 375F for 10 minutes. Shake the chicken skin every 3 minutes to avoid burning.

Nutrition: calories 260, fat 23.3, fiber 0.2, carbs 0.3, protein 11.6

Seafood Balls

Preparation time: 15 minutes
Cooking time: 15 minutes
Servings: 4

Ingredients:
*   1-pound salmon fillet, minced
*   1 egg, beaten
*   3 tablespoons coconut, shredded
*   ½ cup almond flour
*   1 tablespoon avocado oil
*   1 teaspoon dried basil

Directions:
1. In the mixing bowl, mix minced salmon fillet, egg, coconut, almond flour, and dried basil.
2. Make the balls from the fish mixture and put them in the air fryer basket.
3. Sprinkle the balls with avocado oil and cook at 365F for 15 minutes.

Nutrition: calories 268, fat 16.4, fiber 2, carbs 3.9, protein 26.6

Popcorn Balls

Prep time: 10 minutes
Cooking time: 12 minutes
Servings: 6

Ingredients:
• 2 cups ground chicken

• 1 teaspoon Italian seasonings
• 1 egg, beaten
• ¼ cup coconut flour
• 1 tablespoon avocado oil

Directions:
1. Mix the ground chicken with Italian seasonings, egg, and coconut flour.
2. Make the small balls from the chicken mixture (popcorn) and put in the air fryer in one layer.
3. Sprinkle the popcorn balls with avocado oil and cook at 365F for 6 minutes per side.

Nutrition: calories 125, fat 5.4, fiber 1.8, carbs 3, protein 15.1

Parsley Balls

Preparation time: 10 minutes
Cooking time: 8 minutes
Servings: 6

Ingredients:
*   4 pecans, grinded
*   3 tablespoons dried parsley
*   1 teaspoon onion powder
*   1 egg, beaten
*   2 oz Parmesan, grated

Directions:
1. In the mixing bowl, mix pecans with dried basil, onion powder, egg, and Parmesan.
2. Make the balls and put them in the air fryer in one layer.
3. Cook them at 375F for 8 minutes (4 minutes per side).

Nutrition: calories 125, fat 5.2, fiber 2.1, carbs 3.6, protein 15.1

Chicken Pies

Prep time: 15 minutes

Cooking time: 10 minutes
Servings:6

Ingredients:
- 1-pound chicken fillet, boiled
- 1 tablespoon cream cheese
- 1 teaspoon chili powder
- 1 teaspoon garlic powder
- 6 wonton wraps
- 1 egg, beaten
- 1 tablespoon avocado oil

Directions:
1. Shred the chicken fillet and mix it with cream cheese, chili powder, garlic powder, and egg.
2. Then put the chicken mixture on the wonton wraps and roll them.
3. Sprinkle the chicken pies with avocado oil and bake in the air fryer at 375F for 10 minutes.

Nutrition: calories 175, fat 7.3, fiber 0.3, carbs 2.8, protein 23.6

Salmon Bites

Preparation time: 5 minutes
Cooking time: 10 minutes
Servings: 6

Ingredients:
- 1-pound salmon fillet, roughly chopped
- 1 tablespoon avocado oil
- 1 teaspoon dried basil
- 1 teaspoon ground black pepper

Directions:
1. Mix chopped salmon with dried basil and ground black pepper.
2. Put the fish pieces in the air fryer basket and sprinkle with avocado oil.
3. Cook the salmon bites at 375F for 10 minutes.

Nutrition: calories 104, fat 5, fiber 0.2, carbs 0.4, protein 14.7

Eggplant Bites

Prep time: 10 minutes
Cooking time: 25 minutes
Servings:4

Ingredients:
- 1 eggplant, sliced
- ½ teaspoon salt
- 1 teaspoon nutritional yeast

Directions:
1. Sprinkle the sliced eggplant with salt and nutritional yeast.
2. Put it in the air fryer and cook at 360F for 25 minutes.

Nutrition: calories 32, fat 0.3, fiber 4.3, carbs 7.,1 protein 1.5

Cilantro Meatballs

Preparation time: 15 minutes
Cooking time: 20 minutes
Servings: 6

Ingredients:
- 2 cups ground beef
- 1 tablespoon dried cilantro
- 1 egg, beaten
- 1 teaspoon ground black pepper
- Cooking spray

Directions:
1. Spray the air fryer basket with cooking spray.
2. Then mix all remaining ingredients and make the meatballs.
3. Put them in the air fryer and cook at 365F for 20 minutes.

Nutrition: calories 77, fat 4.7, fiber 0.1, carbs 0.3, protein 8

Bacon Rolls

Prep time: 10 minutes
Cooking time: 8 minutes
Servings:5

Ingredients:
- 5 bacon slices
- 3 tablespoons mascarpone
- 1 teaspoon dried oregano

Directions:
1. Preheat the air fryer to 400F.
2. Put the bacon slices inside in one layer and cook for 4 minutes per side.
3. Then cool the bacon slices little and sprinkle with dried oregano.
4. Spread the mascarpone over the bacon slices and roll them.

Nutrition: calories 120, fat 9.2, fiber 0.1, carbs 0.7, protein 8.1

Fish and Seafood

Cheddar Cod

Preparation time: 10 minutes
Cooking time: 15 minutes
Servings: 4

Ingredients:
- 4 cod fillets, boneless
- 1 cup Cheddar cheese, shredded
- 1 teaspoon avocado oil
- ½ teaspoon ground black pepper

Directions:
1. Sprinkle the cod fillets with avocado oil and rub with ground black pepper.
2. Put them in the air fryer basket and top with Cheddar cheese.
3. Cook the fish at 370F for 15 minutes.

Nutrition: calories 206, fat 10.5, fiber 0.1, carbs 0.6, protein 27.1

Bacon Scallops

Prep time: 15 minutes
Cooking time: 7 minutes
Servings: 4

Ingredients:
- 1-pound scallops
- 4 oz bacon, sliced
- 1 teaspoon avocado oil
- 1 teaspoon chili powder

Directions:
1. Wrap the scallops in the bacon and sprinkle with avocado oil and chili powder.
2. Put the scallops in the air fryer and cook them at 400F for 7 minutes.

Nutrition: calories 257, fat 13, fiber 0.3, carbs 3.5, protein 29.6

Cod in Sauce

Preparation time: 5 minutes
Cooking time: 15 minutes
Servings: 2

Ingredients:
- 2 cod fillets, boneless
- ¼ cup heavy cream
- 1 teaspoon ground black pepper
- 1 teaspoon garlic powder
- 1 teaspoon butter, softened
- ½ teaspoon cayenne pepper

Directions:
1. In the mixing bowl, mix heavy cream, ground black pepper, garlic powder, and cayenne pepper.
2. Add butter and whisk the mixture.
3. Then put the cod fillets in the baking pan and top with heavy cream sauce. Put the baking pan in the air fryer.
4. Cook the fish at 375F for 15 minutes.

Nutrition: calories 167, fat 8.6, fiber 0.5, carbs 2.4, protein 20.7

Almond Catfish

Prep time: 10 minutes
Cooking time: 12 minutes
Servings: 4

Ingredients:
- 2-pound catfish fillet
- ½ cup almond flour
- 2 eggs, beaten
- 1 teaspoon salt
- 1 teaspoon avocado oil

Directions:
1. Sprinkle the catfish fillet with salt and dip in the eggs.
2. Then coat the fish in the almond flour and put in the air fryer basket. Sprinkle the fish with avocado oil.
3. Cook the fish for 6 minutes per side at 380F.

Nutrition: calories 423, fat 26.2, fiber 1.6, carbs 3.2, protein 41.1

Lemon Salmon

Preparation time: 10 minutes
Cooking time: 20 minutes
Servings: 4

Ingredients:
- 1-pound salmon fillets, boneless
- 2 tablespoons lemon juice
- 1 teaspoon lemon zest, grated
- 1 teaspoon avocado oil

Directions:
1. Mix lemon juice with lemon zest, and avocado oil.
2. Then carefully rub the salmon fillets with lemon mixture and put it in the air fryer.
3. Cook the salmon for 10 minutes per side at 360F.

Nutrition: calories 154, fat 7.2, fiber 0.1, carbs 0.3, protein 22.1

Onion Shrimps

Prep time: 10 minutes
Cooking time: 5 minutes
Servings: 3

Ingredients:
- 1-pound shrimps, peeled
- 1 teaspoon onion powder
- 1 teaspoon avocado oil
- ½ teaspoon salt

Directions:
1. Sprinkle the shrimps with onion powder, avocado oil, and salt.
2. Put the shrimps in the air fryer and cook at 400F for 5 minutes.

Nutrition: calories 185, fat 2.8, fiber 0.1, carbs 3, protein 34.5

Balsamic Tilapia

Preparation time: 5 minutes
Cooking time: 15 minutes
Servings: 4

Ingredients:
- 4 tilapia fillets, boneless
- 2 tablespoons balsamic vinegar
- 1 teaspoon avocado oil
- 1 teaspoon dried basil

Directions:
1. Sprinkle the tilapia fillets with balsamic vinegar, avocado oil, and dried basil.
2. Then put the fillets in the air fryer basket and cook at 365F for 15 minutes.

Nutrition: calories 96, fat 1.2, fiber 0.1, carbs 0.2, protein 21

Crunchy Red Fish

Prep time: 15 minutes
Cooking time: 8 minutes
Servings: 4

Ingredients:
- 2-pound salmon fillet
- ¼ cup coconut shred
- 2 eggs, beaten
- 1 teaspoon coconut oil

- 1 teaspoon Italian seasonings

Directions:
1. Cut the salmon fillet into servings.
2. Then sprinkle the fish with Italian seasonings and dip in the eggs.
3. After this, coat every salmon fillet in coconut shred and put it in the air fryer.
4. Cook the fish at 375F for 4 minutes per side.

Nutrition: calories 395, fat 22.7, fiber 1, carbs 2.3, protein 46.8

Cumin Catfish

Preparation time: 5 minutes
Cooking time: 15 minutes
Servings: 4

Ingredients:
- 1 tablespoon ground cumin
- 1 tablespoon avocado oil
- ½ teaspoon apple cider vinegar
- 1-pound catfish fillet

Directions:
1. Rub the catfish fillet with ground cumin, avocado oil, and apple cider vinegar/
2. Put the fish in the air fryer and cook at 360F for 15 minutes.

Nutrition: calories 164, fat 9.4, fiber 0.3, carbs 0.9, protein 17.9

Blackened Salmon

Prep time: 10 minutes
Cooking time: 8 minutes
Servings: 2

Ingredients:
- 10 oz salmon fillet
- ½ teaspoon ground coriander

54

- 1 teaspoon ground cumin
- 1 teaspoon dried basil
- 1 tablespoon avocado oil

Directions:
1. In the shallow bowl, mix ground coriander, ground cumin, and dried basil.
2. Then coat the salmon fillet in the spices and sprinkle with avocado oil.
3. Put the fish in the air fryer basket and cook at 395F for 4 minutes per side.

Nutrition: calories 201, fat 9.9, fiber 0.4, carbs 0.9, protein 27.8

Tender Tilapia

Preparation time: 5 minutes
Cooking time: 20 minutes
Servings: 4

Ingredients:
- 4 tilapia fillets, boneless
- 1 tablespoon ghee
- 1 tablespoon apple cider vinegar
- 1 teaspoon dried cilantro

Directions:
1. Sprinkle the tilapia fillets with apple cider vinegar and dried cilantro.
2. Put the fish in the air fryer basket, add ghee, and cook it at 375F for 10 minutes per side.

Nutrition: calories 122, fat 4.2, fiber 0, carbs 0, protein 21

Rosemary Shrimp Skewers

Prep time: 10 minutes
Cooking time: 5 minutes
Servings: 5

Ingredients:

- 4-pounds shrimps, peeled
- 1 tablespoon dried rosemary
- 1 tablespoon avocado oil
- 1 teaspoon apple cider vinegar

Directions:
1. Mix the shrimps with dried rosemary, avocado oil, and apple cider vinegar.
2. Then sting the shrimps into skewers and put in the air fryer.
3. Cook the shrimps at 400F for 5 minutes.

Nutrition: calories 437, fat 6.6, fiber 0.4, carbs 6.1, protein 82.7

Sweet Tilapia Fillets

Preparation time: 5 minutes
Cooking time: 14 minutes
Servings: 4

Ingredients:
- 2 tablespoons Erythritol
- 1 tablespoon apple cider vinegar
- 4 tilapia fillets, boneless
- 1 teaspoon olive oil

Directions:
1. Mix apple cider vinegar with olive oil and Erythritol.
2. Then rub the tilapia fillets with the sweet mixture and put in the air fryer basket in one layer.
3. Cook the fish at 360F for 7 minutes per side.

Nutrition: calories 101, fat 2.2, fiber 0, carbs 0, protein 20

Crab Buns

Prep time: 15 minutes
Cooking time: 20 minutes
Servings: 2

Ingredients:
- 5 oz crab meat, chopped
- 2 eggs, beaten
- 2 tablespoons coconut flour
- ¼ teaspoon baking powder
- ½ teaspoon coconut aminos
- ½ teaspoon ground black pepper
- 1 tablespoon coconut oil, softened

Directions:
1. In the mixing bowl, mix crab meat with eggs, coconut flour, baking powder, coconut aminos, ground black pepper, and coconut oil.
2. Knead the smooth dough and cut it into pieces.
3. Make the buns from the crab mixture and put them in the air fryer basket.
4. Cook the crab buns at 365F for 20 minutes.

Nutrition: calories 217, fat 13.2, fiber 3.2, carbs 7.3, protein 15.5

Chili and Oregano Tilapia

Preparation time: 5 minutes
Cooking time: 20 minutes
Servings: 4

Ingredients:
- 4 tilapia fillets, boneless
- 1 teaspoon chili flakes
- 1 teaspoon dried oregano
- 1 tablespoon avocado oil
- 1 teaspoon mustard

Directions:
1. Rub the tilapia fillets with chili flakes, dried oregano, avocado oil, and mustard and put in the air fryer.
2. Cook it for 10 minutes per side at 360F.

Nutrition: calories 103, fat 1.7, fiber 0.4, carbs 0.8, protein 21.3

Creamy Haddock

Prep time: 10 minutes
Cooking time: 8 minutes
Servings: 4

Ingredients:
- 1-pound haddock fillet
- 1 teaspoon cayenne pepper
- 1 teaspoon salt
- 1 teaspoon coconut oil
- ½ cup heavy cream

Directions:
1. Grease the baking pan with coconut oil.
2. Then put haddock fillet inside and sprinkle it with cayenne pepper, salt, and heavy cream.
3. Put the baking pan in the air fryer basket and cook at 7375F for 8 minutes.

Nutrition: calories 190, fat 7.8, fiber 0.1, carbs 0.7, protein 27.9

Jalapeno Cod

Preparation time: 5 minutes
Cooking time: 14 minutes
Servings: 4

Ingredients:
- 4 cod fillets, boneless
- 1 jalapeno, minced
- 1 tablespoon avocado oil
- ½ teaspoon minced garlic

Directions:
1. In the shallow bowl, mix minced jalapeno, avocado oil, and minced garlic.

2. Put the cod fillets in the air fryer basket in one layer and top with minced jalapeno mixture.
3. Cook the fish at 365F for 7 minutes per side.

Nutrition: calories 96, fat 1.5, fiber 0.3, carbs 0.5, protein 20.1

Stuffed Mackerel

Prep time: 15 minutes
Cooking time: 20 minutes
Servings: 5

Ingredients:
- 1-pound mackerel, trimmed
- 1 bell pepper, chopped
- ½ cup spinach, chopped
- 1 tablespoon avocado oil
- 1 teaspoon ground black pepper
- 1 teaspoon keto tomato paste

Directions:
1. In the mixing bowl, mix bell pepper with spinach, ground black pepper, and tomato paste.
2. Fill the mackerel with spinach mixture.
3. Then brush the fish with avocado oil and put it in the air fryer.
4. Cook the fish at 365F for 20 minutes.

Nutrition: calories 252, fat 16.6, fiber 0.7, carbs 0.5, protein 22.1

Cod Pan

Preparation time: 5 minutes
Cooking time: 12 minutes
Servings: 4

Ingredients:
- 1-pound cod fillet, chopped
- 1 teaspoon coconut oil

- 1 teaspoon chili flakes
- ½ teaspoon cayenne pepper
- 1 teaspoon dried cilantro
- ¼ teaspoon ground nutmeg

Directions:
1. Rub the cod fillet with coconut oil, chili flakes, cayenne pepper, dried cilantro, and ground nutmeg.
2. Put the fillets in the air fryer and cook for 6 minutes per side at 365F.

Nutrition: calories 102, fat 2.2, fiber 0.1, carbs 0.2, protein 20.3

Golden Sardines

Prep time: 15 minutes
Cooking time: 10 minutes
Servings: 5

Ingredients:
- 12 oz sardines, trimmed, cleaned
- 1 cup coconut flour
- 1 tablespoon coconut oil
- 1 teaspoon salt

Directions:
1. Sprinkle the sardines with salt and coat in the coconut flour.
2. Then grease the air fryer basket with coconut oil and put the sardines inside.
3. Cook them at 385F for 10 minutes.

Nutrition: calories 165, fat 10.5, fiber 0, carbs 0.3, protein 16.8

Basil Shrimps

Preparation time: 5 minutes
Cooking time: 12 minutes
Servings: 4

Ingredients:
- 1 tablespoon avocado oil

- ½ teaspoon salt
- 1 teaspoon dried basil
- 1-pound shrimps, peeled

Directions:
1. Mix shrimps with salt, dried basil, and avocado oil.
2. Put them in the air fryer in one layer and cook at 365F for 12 minutes.

Nutrition: calories 139, fat 2.4, fiber 0.2, carbs 1.9, protein 25.9

Bacon Halibut

Prep time: 15 minutes
Cooking time: 10 minutes
Servings: 4

Ingredients:
- 24 oz halibut steaks (6 oz each fillet)
- 1 teaspoon avocado oil
- 1 teaspoon ground black pepper
- 4 oz bacon, sliced

Directions:
1. Sprinkle the halibut steaks with avocado oil and ground black pepper.
2. Then wrap the fish in the bacon slices and put in the air fryer.
3. Cook the fish at 390F for 5 minutes per side.

Nutrition: calories 266, fat 14, fiber 0.2, carbs 0.8, protein 33.6

Provolone Salmon

Preparation time: 5 minutes
Cooking time: 15 minutes
Servings: 4

Ingredients:
- 1-pound salmon fillet, chopped
- 2 oz Provolone, grated
- 1 teaspoon avocado oil

- ¼ teaspoon ground paprika

Directions:
1. Sprinkle the salmon fillets with avocado oil and put in the air fryer.
2. Then sprinkle the fish with ground paprika and top with Provolone cheese.
3. Cook the fish at 360F for 15 minutes.

Nutrition: calories 202, fat 10.9, fiber 0.1, carbs 0.4, protein 25.7

Cheesy Shrimp Bake

Prep time: 15 minutes
Cooking time: 5 minutes
Servings: 4

Ingredients:
- 14 oz shrimps, peeled
- 1 egg, beaten
- ½ cup of coconut milk
- 1 cup Cheddar cheese, shredded
- ½ teaspoon coconut oil
- 1 teaspoon ground coriander

Directions:
1. In the mixing bowl, mix shrimps with egg, coconut milk, Cheddar cheese, coconut oil, and ground coriander.
2. Then put the mixture in the baking ramekins and put in the air fryer.
3. Cook the shrimps at 400F for 5 minutes.

Nutrition: calories 321, fat 19.9, fiber 0.7, carbs 3.6, protein 31.7

Lime Salmon

Preparation time: 5 minutes
Cooking time: 20 minutes
Servings: 4

Ingredients:
- 1-pound salmon, chopped
- 1 tablespoon lime juice
- 1 teaspoon avocado oil
- 1 teaspoon lime zest, grated
- ¼ teaspoon ground nutmeg

Directions:
1. Rub the salmon with lime juice, lime zest, ground nutmeg, avocado oil.
2. Put the salmon in the air fryer and cook for 20 minutes at 360F.

Nutrition: calories 154, fat 7.2, fiber 0.2, carbs 0.7, protein 22.1

Nuggets

Prep time: 10 minutes
Cooking time: 10 minutes
Servings: 4

Ingredients:
- ¼ cup coconut shred
- 3 tablespoons almond flour
- 1 teaspoon salt
- 3 eggs, beaten
- 10 oz cod fillet
- 1 teaspoon avocado oil

Directions:
1. Cut the cod fillets into nuggets and sprinkle with salt.
2. Then dip the fish in eggs and coat in almond flour.
3. After this, dip the fish in the eggs again and coat in the coconut shred.
4. Then put the nuggets in the air fryer and sprinkle with avocado oil.
5. Cook the nuggets for 5 minutes per side at 375F.

Nutrition: calories 275, fat 19.6, fiber 3.3, carbs 6.8, protein 21.2

Mustard Tilapia

Preparation time: 10 minutes
Cooking time: 14 minutes
Servings: 4

Ingredients:
- 1 cup Monterey Jack cheese, grated
- 4 tilapia fillets
- ¼ teaspoon ground cumin
- 1 tablespoon Dijon mustard

Directions:
1. Rub the tilapia fillets with ground cumin and Dijon mustard.
2. Put the fish in the air fryer in one layer and top with cheese.
3. Cook the tilapia for 14 minutes at 370F.

Nutrition: calories 201, fat 9.8, fiber 0.1, carbs 0.5, protein 28.1

Turmeric Cod

Prep time: 10 minutes
Cooking time: 7 minutes
Servings: 2

Ingredients:
- 12 oz cod fillet
- 1 teaspoon ground turmeric
- 1 teaspoon chili flakes
- 1 tablespoon coconut oil, melted
- ½ teaspoon salt

Directions:
1. Mix coconut oil with ground turmeric, chili flakes, and salt.
2. Then mix cod fillet with ground turmeric and put in the air fryer basket.
3. Cook the cod at 385F for 7 minutes.

Nutrition: calories 199, fat 8.4, fiber 0.2, carbs 0.8, protein 30.5

Garlic Salmon Cubes

Preparation time: 5 minutes
Cooking time: 15 minutes
Servings: 4

Ingredients:
- 2-pounds salmon, cubed
- 1 teaspoon minced garlic
- ½ teaspoon garlic powder
- 1 tablespoon ghee, melted
- ½ teaspoon dried dill
- ½ teaspoon dried parsley

Directions:
1. Mix salmon cubes with minced garlic, garlic powder, dried dill, and parsley.
2. Put the ghee in the air fryer and add salmon.
3. Cook the salmon at 370F for 15 minutes. Shake the fish every 5 minutes.

Nutrition: calories 331, fat 17.2, fiber 0.1, carbs 0.6, protein 44.1

Chili Cod

Prep time: 15 minutes
Cooking time: 9 minutes
Servings: 2

Ingredients:
- 1 chili pepper, chopped
- 12 oz cod fillet, sliced
- 1 teaspoon avocado oil
- ½ teaspoon ground cinnamon

Directions:
1. Sprinkle the cod fillet with avocado oil and put it in the air fryer basket.

2. Then top it with chili pepper and ground cinnamon.
3. Cook the fish at 375F for 9 minutes.

Nutrition: calories 142, fat 1.8, fiber 0.5, carbs 0.8, protein 30.5

Sautéed Fish with Endives

Preparation time: 5 minutes
Cooking time: 20 minutes
Servings: 4

Ingredients:
- 2 endives, shredded
- 1-pound salmon fillet, chopped
- 1 tablespoon ghee
- 1 teaspoon ground coriander
- ¼ cup coconut cream

Directions:
1. Put all ingredients in the air fryer and shake gently.
2. Close the lid and cook the meal ay 360F for 20 minutes. Shake the fish every 5 minutes.

Nutrition: calories 223, fat 13.9, fiber 2.3, carbs 3, protein 23.2

Coconut Aminos Cod
Prep time: 10 minutes
Cooking time: 9 minutes
Servings:6

Ingredients:
- 2-pound salmon fillet, chopped
- 1 teaspoon Erythritol
- 1 tablespoon coconut aminos
- ½ teaspoon dried basil
- 1 tablespoon avocado oil

Directions:
1. Mix salmon with Erythritol, coconut aminos, dried basil, and avocado oil.

2. Marinate the fish for 5 minutes.
3. Then put the mixture in the air fryer and cook for 9 minutes at 360F.

Nutrition: calories 204, fat 9.6, fiber 0.1, carbs 0.3, protein 29.4

Tuna Skewers

Preparation time: 10 minutes
Cooking time: 12 minutes
Servings: 4

Ingredients:
- 1-pound tuna steaks, boneless and cubed
- 1 tablespoon mustard
- 1 tablespoon avocado oil
- 1 tablespoon apple cider vinegar

Directions:
1. Mix avocado oil with mustard and apple cider vinegar.
2. Then brush tuna steaks with mustard mixture and put in the air fryer basket.
3. Cook the fish at 360F for 6 minutes per side.

Nutrition: calories 227, fat 8.4, fiber 0.6, carbs 1.2, protein 34.7

Onion Mussels

Prep time: 10 minutes
Cooking time: 2 minute
Servings:5

Ingredients:
- 2-pounds mussels, cleaned, peeled
- 1 teaspoon onion powder
- 1 teaspoon ground cumin
- 1 tablespoon avocado oil
- ¼ cup apple cider vinegar

Directions:

1. Mix mussels with onion powder, ground cumin, avocado oil, and apple cider vinegar.
2. Put the mussels in the air fryer and cook at 395F for 2 minutes.

Nutrition: calories 166, fat 4.5, fiber 0.2, carbs 7.6, protein 21.7

Tomatillos Cod

Preparation time: 10 minutes
Cooking time: 15 minutes
Servings: 4

Ingredients:
- 2 oz tomatillos, chopped
- 1-pound cod fillet, roughly chopped
- 1 tablespoon avocado oil
- 1 tablespoon lemon juice
- 1 teaspoon keto tomato paste

Directions:
1. Mix avocado oil with lemon juice and tomato paste.
2. Then mix cod fillet with tomato mixture and put in the air fryer.
3. Add lemon juice and tomatillos.
4. Cook the cod at 370F for 15 minutes.

Nutrition: calories 102, fat 1.6, fiber 0.5, carbs 1.4, protein 20.5

Tender Salmon
Prep time: 10 minutes
Cooking time: 9 minute
Servings: 3

Ingredients:
- 1-pound salmon
- 1 teaspoon dried rosemary
- 2 tablespoons olive oil
- ½ teaspoon salt

Directions:

1. Sprinkle the salmon with dried rosemary, olive oil, and salt.
2. Put the salmon in the air fryer and cook at 390F for 9 minutes.

Nutrition: calories 281, fat 18.7, fiber 0.2, carbs 0.3, protein 29.4

Roasted Tilapia

Preparation time: 5 minutes
Cooking time: 20 minutes
Servings: 4

Ingredients:
- 4 tilapia fillets, boneless and halved
- 1 tablespoon avocado oil
- 1 teaspoon ground turmeric

Directions:
1. Sprinkle the tilapia fillets with avocado oil and ground turmeric.
2. Put it in the air fryer and cook at 365F for 10 minutes per side.

Nutrition: calories 100, fat 1.5, fiber 0.3, carbs 0.6, protein 21.1

Lime Lobster Tail

Prep time: 10 minutes
Cooking time: 6 minutes
Servings: 4

Ingredients:
- 4 lobster tails, peeled
- 2 tablespoons lime juice
- ½ teaspoon dried basil
- ½ teaspoon coconut oil, melted

Directions:
1. Mix lobster tails with lime juice, dried basil, and coconut oil.
2. Put the lobster tails in the air fryer and cook at 380F for 6 minutes.

Nutrition: calories 83, fat 1.3, fiber 0, carbs 0.5, protein 16.2

Shrimp Vinaigrette

Preparation time: 5 minutes
Cooking time: 12 minutes
Servings: 4

Ingredients:
- 1-pound shrimps, peeled
- 3 tablespoons apple cider vinegar
- 1 teaspoon ground black pepper
- 1 teaspoon dried dill
- 1 jalapeno, chopped
- 1 tablespoon avocado oil

Directions:
1. Mix shrimps with all remaining ingredients and put in the air fryer.
2. Cook the shrimps at 350F for 12 minutes.

Nutrition: calories 145, fat 2.4, fiber 0.4, carbs 2.7, protein 26

Oregano Fish Fingers

Prep time: 15 minutes
Cooking time: 9 minute
Servings:4

Ingredients:
- 1-pound tilapia fillet
- ½ cup coconut flour
- 2 eggs, beaten
- ½ teaspoon ground paprika
- 1 teaspoon dried oregano
- 1 teaspoon avocado oil

Directions:
1. Cut the tilapia fillets into fingers and sprinkle with ground paprika and dried oregano.

2. Then dip the tilapia fingers in eggs and coat in the coconut flour.
3. Sprinkle fish fingers with avocado oil and cook in the air fryer at 370F for 9 minutes.

Nutrition: calories 188, fat 5.4, fiber 5.3, carbs 8.6, protein 26

Parsley and Cilantro Shrimp

Preparation time: 5 minutes
Cooking time: 12 minutes
Servings: 4

Ingredients:
- 1-pound shrimp, peeled and deveined
- 1 teaspoon dried parsley
- 1 teaspoon dried cilantro
- 1 tablespoon olive oil
- ½ teaspoon salt

Directions:
1. Mix parsley with shrimps, cilantro, salt, and olive oil.
2. Put the shrimp mixture in the air fryer basket and cook at 360F for 12 minutes.

Nutrition: calories 165, fat 5.4, fiber 0, carbs 1.7, protein 25.8

Allspices Salmon with Spices

Prep time: 10 minutes
Cooking time: 15 minutes
Servings: 4

Ingredients:
- 1 teaspoon allspices
- 1-pound salmon
- 1 tablespoon avocado oil

Directions:

1. Rub the salmon with allspices and sprinkle with avocado oil.
2. Put the salmon in the air fryer basket and cook at 360F for 15 minutes.

Nutrition: calories 156, fat 7.5, fiber 0.3, carbs 0.6, protein 22.1

Shrimp and Swiss Chard Bowl

Preparation time: 10 minutes
Cooking time: 10 minutes
Servings: 4

Ingredients:
- 1-pound shrimp, peeled and deveined
- ½ teaspoon smoked paprika
- ½ cup Swiss chard, chopped
- 2 tablespoons apple cider vinegar
- 1 tablespoon coconut oil
- ¼ cup heavy cream

Directions:
1. Mix shrimps with smoked paprika and apple cider vinegar.
2. Put the shrimps in the air fryer and add coconut oil.
3. Cook the shrimps at 350F for 10 minutes.
4. Then mix cooked shrimps with remaining ingredients and carefully mix.

Nutrition: calories 193, fat 8.1, fiber 0.2, carbs 2.3, protein 26.1

Rosemary Scallops

Prep time: 10 minutes
Cooking time: 6 minutes
Servings: 4

Ingredients:
- 12 oz scallops
- 1 tablespoon dried rosemary
- ½ teaspoon Pink salt
- 1 tablespoon avocado oil

Directions:
1. Sprinkle scallops with dried rosemary, Pink salt, and avocado oil.
2. Then put the scallops in the air fryer basket in one layer and cook at 400F 6 minutes.

Nutrition: calories 82, fat 1.2, fiber 0.5, carbs 2.7, protein 14.4

Italian Style Shrimp

Preparation time: 3 minutes
Cooking time: 5 minutes
Servings: 4

Ingredients:
- 1-pound shrimp, peeled
- 1 tablespoon avocado oil
- 1 tablespoon Italian seasonings

Directions:
1. Put the shrimps in the air fryer basket and sprinkle with avocado oil and Italian seasonings.
2. Cook the shrimps at 400F for 5 minutes.

Nutrition: calories 150, fat 3.4, fiber 0.2, carbs 2.3, protein 25.9

Seafood Salad

Prep time: 10 minutes
Cooking time: 5 minutes
Servings: 4

Ingredients:
- ½ cup mozzarella, shredded
- 1 tablespoon apple cider vinegar
- 1 teaspoon white pepper
- 1 cup lettuce, chopped

- 1-pound shrimps, peeled
- 1 teaspoon avocado oil
- 1 teaspoon chili powder

Directions:
1. Mix shrimps with white pepper and apple cider vinegar.
2. Cook the shrimps in the air fryer at 400F for 5 minutes.
3. Then put the shrimps in the salad bowl.
4. Add all remaining ingredients and shake the salad.

Nutrition: calories 152, fat 2.9, fiber 0.5, carbs 3.1, protein 27

Hot Cod

Preparation time: 5 minutes
Cooking time: 15 minutes
Servings: 4

Ingredients:
- 4 cod fillets, boneless
- 1 tablespoon keto hot sauce
- 1 tablespoon avocado oil
- ½ teaspoon ground cinnamon

Directions:
1. Sprinkle the cod fillets with hot sauce, avocado oil, and ground cinnamon.
2. Then put the fish in the air fryer basket and cook it for 15 minutes at 350F.

Nutrition: calories 96, fat 1.5, fiber 0.3, carbs 0.5, protein 20.1

Cajun Shrimps

Prep time: 10 minutes
Cooking time: 6 minutes
Servings: 4

Ingredients:
- 1-pound shrimps, peeled
- 1 teaspoon Cajun seasonings
- 1 teaspoon mascarpone
- ½ teaspoon salt
- 1 teaspoon olive oil

Directions:
1. Mix shrimps with Cajun seasonings, salt, and olive oil.
2. Put the shrimps in the air fryer and cook them at 395F for 6 minutes.
3. Then transfer the shrimps in the bowl and sprinkle with mascarpone.

Nutrition: calories 147, fat 3.3, fiber 0, carbs 1.8, protein 26

Crunchy Shrimps

Preparation time: 5 minutes
Cooking time: 12 minutes
Servings: 4

Ingredients:
- 1-pound shrimp, peeled
- 3 tablespoons coconut shred
- 2 eggs, beaten
- 1 teaspoon salt

Directions:
1. Mix shrimps with salt.
2. Then dip every shrimp in the eggs and coat in the coconut shred.
3. Put the shrimps in the air fryer and cook at 375F for 12 minutes.

Nutrition: calories 204, fat 7.9, fiber 0.8, carbs 3.4, protein 28.6

Tilapia Fritters

Prep time: 15 minutes
Cooking time: 12 minutes
Servings: 4

Ingredients:
- 1-pound tilapia fillet, diced
- 3 tablespoons coconut flour
- ¼ cup cauliflower, shredded
- 1 egg, beaten
- 1 teaspoon ground black pepper
- ¼ teaspoon ground paprika

Directions:
1. In the mixing bowl, mix diced tilapia fillet, coconut flour, cauliflower, egg, ground black pepper, ground paprika.
2. Make the fritters from the tilapia mixture and put in the air fryer in one layer.
3. Cook the fritters at 365F for 6 minutes per side.

Nutrition: calories 135, fat 2.7, fiber 2.6, carbs 4.6, protein 23.4

Salmon Fritters

Preparation time: 15 minutes
Cooking time: 12 minutes
Servings: 4

Ingredients:
- 2 tablespoons almond flour
- 1 zucchini, grated
- 1 egg, beaten
- 6 oz salmon fillet, diced
- 1 teaspoon avocado oil
- ½ teaspoon ground black pepper

Directions:
1. Mix almond flour with zucchini, egg, salmon, and ground black pepper.
2. Then make the fritters from the salmon mixture.
3. Sprinkle the air fryer basket with avocado oil and put the fritters inside.
4. Cook the fritters at 375F for 6 minutes per side.

Nutrition: calories 103, fat 5.6, fiber 1, carbs 2.7, protein 11

Hot Calamari

Prep time: 10 minutes
Cooking time: 6 minutes
Servings: 2

Ingredients:
- 10 oz calamari, trimmed
- 2 tablespoons keto hot sauce
- 1 tablespoon avocado oil

Directions:
1. Slice the calamari and sprinkle with avocado oil.
2. Put the calamari in the air fryer and cook at 400F for 3 minutes per side.
3. Then transfer the calamari in the serving plate and sprinkle with hot sauce.

Nutrition: calories 36, fat 2, fiber 0.4, carbs 1.7, protein 2.7

Stuffed Salmon

Preparation time: 15 minutes
Cooking time: 15 minutes
Servings: 4

Ingredients:
- 1-pound salmon fillet
- 4 kalamata olives, sliced
- 1 teaspoon avocado oil
- 1 teaspoon Italian seasonings
- 2 oz Mozzarella, shredded

Directions:
1. Make the cut in the salmon in the shape of the pocket.
2. The fill the salmon cut with olives and mozzarella.

3. Secure the cut with the help of the toothpick and sprinkle the salmon with Italian seasonings and avocado oil.
4. Cook the salmon in the air fryer basket and cook it at 380F for 15 minutes.

Nutrition: calories 200, fat 10.5, fiber 0.2, carbs 1, protein 26.1

Lemon Crawfish

Prep time: 10 minutes
Cooking time: 5 minutes
Servings: 4

Ingredients:
- 1-pound crawfish
- 1 tablespoon olive oil
- 2 tablespoons lemon juice

Directions:
1. Put the crawfish in the air fryer and cook at 370F for 5 minutes.
2. Then remove the crawfish from the air fryer and sprinkle with olive oil and lemon juice.

Nutrition: calories 130, fat 5, fiber 0, carbs 0.2, protein 19.9

Shrimp Cakes

Preparation time: 15 minutes
Cooking time: 15 minutes
Servings: 4

Ingredients:
- 1-pound shrimp, peeled, chopped
- 3 tablespoons coconut flour
- 1 egg, beaten
- 1 zucchini, grated
- 1 teaspoon avocado oil

Directions:

1. Mix chopped shrimps with coconut flour, egg, and grated zucchini.
2. Brush the air fryer basket with avocado oil.
3. Then make the shrimp cakes and put in the air fryer.
4. Cook them for 375F for 15 minutes.

Nutrition: calories 182, fat 3.8, fiber 2.8, carbs 7.3, protein 28.6

Tuna Boats

Prep time: 15 minutes
Cooking time: 12 minutes
Servings: 2

Ingredients:
- 1 zucchini, trimmed, halved
- 6 oz tuna, canned
- 1 teaspoon dried parsley
- 2 oz Parmesan, grated

Directions:
1. Remove the flesh from the zucchini to get the shape of the boards.
2. Then mix tuna with dried parsley and Parmesan.
3. Fill the zucchini boats with tuna mixture and put in the air fryer basket.
4. Cook the meal at 380F for 12 minutes.

Nutrition: calories 265, fat 13.1, fiber 1.1, carbs 4.3, protein 32.9

Clove Shrimps

Preparation time: 5 minutes
Cooking time: 12 minutes
Servings: 4

Ingredients:
- 1-pound shrimp, peeled and deveined

- 1 tablespoon avocado oil
- 1 teaspoon ground clove

Directions:
1. Mix shrimps with avocado oil and ground clove.
2. Put the shrimps in the air fryer and cook the shrimps at 350F for 12 minutes.

Nutrition: calories 141, fat 2.5, fiber 0.3, carbs 2.2, protein 25.6

Roasted Shrimps

Prep time: 10 minutes
Cooking time: 5 minutes
Servings: 3

Ingredients:
- 2 bell peppers, sliced
- 1 tablespoon apple cider vinegar
- 1 teaspoon fajita seasonings
- 1 teaspoon onion powder
- 1 tablespoon avocado oil
- 1-pound shrimps, peeled

Directions:
1. In the shallow bowl, mix apple cider vinegar, fajita seasonings, onion powder, and avocado oil.
2. Then mix shrimps with the spice mixture and put in the air fryer.
3. Cook the shrimps for 5 minutes at 400F.
4. Transfer the shrimps in the serving plate and top with bell peppers.

Nutrition: calories 219, fat 3.4, fiber 1.3, carbs 10, protein 35.4

Salmon Rice

Preparation time: 10 minutes
Cooking time: 25 minutes
Servings: 4

Ingredients:
- 1-pound salmon fillet, diced
- 1 cup cauliflower, shredded
- 1 tablespoon dried cilantro
- 1 tablespoon coconut oil, melted
- 1 teaspoon ground turmeric
- ¼ cup coconut cream

Directions:
1. Mix salmon with cauliflower, dried cilantro, ground turmeric, coconut cream, and coconut oil.
2. Transfer the salmon mixture in the air fryer and cook the meal at 350F for 25 minutes. Stir the meal every 5 minutes to avoid the burning.

Nutrition: calories 222, fat 14.1, fiber 1.1, carbs 2.5, protein 22.9

Parm Mackerel

Prep time: 10 minutes
Cooking time: 7 minutes
Servings: 2

Ingredients:
- 12 oz mackerel fillet
- 2 oz Parmesan, grated
- 1 teaspoon ground coriander
- 1 tablespoon olive oil

Directions:
1. Sprinkle the mackerel fillet with olive oil and put it in the air fryer basket.
2. Top the fish with ground coriander and Parmesan.
3. Cook the fish at 390F for 7 minutes.

Nutrition: calories 597, fat 43.4, fiber 0, carbs 1, protein 49.7

Mint Sardines

Preparation time: 10 minutes
Cooking time: 16 minutes
Servings: 4

Ingredients:
- 1-pound sardines, trimmed
- 1 teaspoon dried mint
- 1 teaspoon olive oil
- ½ teaspoon salt
- ½ teaspoon ground black pepper

Directions:
1. Sprinkle the sardines with dried mint, olive oil, salt, and ground black pepper.
2. Put the sardines in the air fryer basket and cook them at 375F for 8 minutes per side.

Nutrition: calories 247, fat 14.2, fiber 0.1, carbs 0.2, protein 28

Coconut Mackerel

Prep time: 10 minutes
Cooking time: 6 minutes
Servings: 4

Ingredients:
- 2-pound mackerel fillet
- 1 cup coconut cream
- 1 teaspoon ground coriander
- 1 teaspoon cumin seeds
- 1 garlic clove, peeled, chopped

Directions:
1. Chop the mackerel roughly and sprinkle it with coconut cream, ground coriander, cumin seeds, and garlic.
2. Then put the fish in the air fryer and cook at 400F for 6 minutes.

Nutrition: calories 735, fat 54.8, fiber 1.4, carbs 3.8, protein 55.6

Trout with Herbs de Provance

Preparation time: 10 minutes
Cooking time: 20 minutes
Servings: 4

Ingredients:
- 2-pound trout fillet
- 1 tablespoon olive oil
- 1 tablespoon Herbs de Provance

Directions:
1. Rub the trout with Herbs de Provance and sprinkle with olive oil.
2. Put the fish in the air fryer basket and cook at 375F for 10 minutes per side.

Nutrition: calories 461, fat 22.7, fiber 0, carbs 0, protein 60.4

Fennel Tilapia

Prep time: 15 minutes
Cooking time: 10 minutes
Servings: 4

Ingredients:
- 2-pound tilapia fillet
- 1 teaspoon fennel seeds
- 1 tablespoon avocado oil
- ½ teaspoon lime zest, grated
- 1 tablespoon coconut aminos

Directions:
1. In the shallow bowl, mix fennel seeds with avocado oil, lime zest, and coconut aminos.
2. Then brush the tilapia fillet with fennel seeds and put in the air fryer.
3. Cook the fish at 380F for 10 minutes.

Nutrition: calories 194, fat 2.6, fiber 0.4, carbs 0.8, protein 42.3

Spring Salmon

Preparation time: 5 minutes
Cooking time: 12 minutes
Servings: 4

Ingredients:
- 1-pound salmon fillet
- 2 oz spring onions
- ½ cup heavy cream
- 1 teaspoon ground black pepper
- ½ teaspoon dried rosemary
- ¼ teaspoon salt

Directions:
1. Mix salmon fillet with ground black pepper, salt, and dried rosemary.
2. Then put fish in the air fryer basket and add heavy cream.
3. Cook the fish for 10 minutes at 380F.
4. Then add spring onions and cook the meal for 2 minutes more.

Nutrition: calories 208, fat 12.6, fiber 0.6, carbs 1.9, protein 22.6

Poultry

Gai Yang Chicken

Prep time: 10 minutes
Cooking time: 65 minutes
Servings: 4

Ingredients:
- 2-pounds Cornish hens, roughly chopped
- 2 tablespoons Gai yang spices
- 1 tablespoon avocado oil

Directions:
1. Rub the hens with spices carefully.
2. Then sprinkle the hens with avocado oil and put in the air fryer.
3. Cook the meal at 370F for 65 minutes.

Nutrition: calories 309, fat 9.2, fiber 0.2, carbs 0.2, protein 52.9

Smoked Paprika Chicken

Preparation time: 10 minutes
Cooking time: 20 minutes
Servings: 4

Ingredients:
- 2-pounds chicken breast, skinless, boneless
- 1 tablespoon smoked paprika
- 1 teaspoon coconut oil, melted
- 1 tablespoon apple cider vinegar

Directions:
1. In the shallow bowl, mix coconut oil with apple cider vinegar, and smoked paprika.
2. Carefully brush the chicken breast with smoked paprika mixture.
3. Then put the chicken in the air fryer and cook it at 375F for 20 minutes. Flip the chicken on another side after 10 minutes of cooking.

Nutrition: calories 274, fat 7, fiber 0.7, carbs 1, protein 48.3

Almond Meatballs

Prep time: 10 minutes
Cooking time: 12 minutes
Servings: 6

Ingredients:
- 16 oz ground chicken
- ½ cup almond flour
- 1 teaspoon salt
- 1 teaspoon ground black pepper
- 1 tablespoon avocado oil

Directions:
1. Mix ground chicken with almond flour, salt, and ground black pepper.
2. After this, make the meatballs and put them in the air fryer in one layer.
3. Sprinkle the meatballs with avocado oil and cook at 370F for 12 minutes.

Nutrition: calories 204, fat 10.3, fiber 1.2, carbs 2.4, protein 23.9

Lemon Chicken Thighs

Preparation time: 5 minutes
Cooking time: 30 minutes
Servings: 4

Ingredients:
- 8 chicken thighs, boneless, skinless
- 1 tablespoon lemon zest, grated
- 2 tablespoons lemon juice
- 1 teaspoon avocado oil
- 1 teaspoon salt

Directions:
1. Rub the chicken thighs with lemon zest, lemon juice, avocado oil, and salt.
2. Put the chicken thighs in the air fryer basket and cook at 370F for 30 minutes.
3. Flip the chicken thighs on another side after 15 minutes of cooking.

Nutrition: calories 559, fat 21.9, fiber 0.2, carbs 0.5, protein 84.6

Coriander Chicken Drumsticks

Prep time: 10 minutes
Cooking time: 20 minutes
Servings: 6

Ingredients:
- 6 chicken drumsticks
- 1 tablespoon coconut oil, melted
- 1 tablespoon ground coriander
- 1 teaspoon garlic powder
- ½ teaspoon salt

Directions:
1. Sprinkle the chicken drumsticks with ground coriander, salt, and garlic powder.
2. Then sprinkle the chicken drumsticks with coconut oil and put it in the air fryer.
3. Cook the meal at 375F for 20 minutes.

Nutrition: calories 99, fat 4.9, fiber 0.0, carbs 0.4, protein 12.7

Garlic Chicken Wings

Preparation time: 10 minutes
Cooking time: 30 minutes
Servings: 4

Ingredients:

- 2 pounds of chicken wings
- 1 tablespoon coconut oil, softened
- 1 tablespoon garlic powder
- ¼ cup apple cider vinegar

Directions:
1. Mix chicken wings with coconut oil, garlic powder, and apple cider vinegar.
2. Put them in the air fryer basket and cook at 365F for 30 minutes.

Nutrition: calories 470, fat 20.2, fiber 0.2, carbs 1.7, protein 66

Sweet Chicken Wings
Prep time: 10 minutes
Cooking time: 16 minutes
Servings: 4

Ingredients:
- 1-pound chicken wings
- 1 tablespoon taco seasonings
- 1 tablespoon Erythritol
- 1 tablespoon coconut oil, melted

Directions:
1. Mix chicken wings with taco seasonings, Erythritol, and coconut oil.
2. Put the chicken wings in the air fryer basket and cook them at 380F for 16 minutes.

Nutrition: calories 250, fat 11.8, fiber 0, carbs 3.8, protein 33.1

Basil Chicken Wings

Preparation time: 5 minutes
Cooking time: 30 minutes
Servings: 4

Ingredients:

- 2 pounds of chicken wings
- 1 tablespoon dried basil
- 1 teaspoon salt
- 1 tablespoon avocado oil

Directions:
1. Sprinkle the chicken wings with dried basil, salt, and avocado oil.
2. Put the chicken wings in the air fryer basket and cook at 360F for 30 minutes.

Nutrition: calories 436, fat 17.3, fiber 0.2, carbs 0.2, protein 65.7

Coated Chicken

Prep time: 15 minutes
Cooking time: 20 minutes
Servings: 6

Ingredients:
- 3-pounds chicken breast, skinless, boneless
- 1 tablespoon coconut shred
- 2 tablespoons pork rinds
- 1 teaspoon ground black pepper
- 2 eggs, beaten
- 1 tablespoon avocado oil

Directions:
1. In the shallow bowl, mix coconut shred with pork rinds, and ground black pepper.
2. Then cut the chicken breasts into 6 servings and dip in the eggs.
3. Coat the chicken in the coconut shred mixture and put it in the air fryer basket.
4. Then sprinkle the chicken with avocado oil and cook at 380F for 20 minutes.

Nutrition: calories 305, fat 8.7, fiber 0.3, carbs 1.1, protein 52.2

Ginger Drumsticks

Preparation time: 5 minutes
Cooking time: 20 minutes

Servings: 4

Ingredients:
- 1 teaspoon ground ginger
- ½ teaspoon ground cinnamon
- 1 tablespoon olive oil
- ½ teaspoon onion powder
- 2-pounds chicken drumsticks

Directions:
1. Mix the chicken drumsticks with onion powder, olive oil, ground cinnamon, and ground ginger.
2. Put them in the air fryer basket and cook at 380F for 20 minutes.

Nutrition: calories 417, fat 16.5, fiber 0.2, carbs 0.8, protein 62.5

BBQ Wings

Prep time: 10 minutes
Cooking time: 18 minutes
Servings: 4

Ingredients:
- 2-pound chicken wings
- 1 cup keto BBQ sauce
- 1 teaspoon olive oil

Directions:
1. Mix BBQ sauce with olive oil.
2. Brush the chicken wings carefully with the BQ sauce mixture and put it in the air fryer.
3. Cook the chicken wings for 9 minutes per side at 375F.

Nutrition: calories 531, fat 18, fiber 0, carbs 0.2, protein 65.6

Asparagus Chicken

Preparation time: 15 minutes
Cooking time: 25 minutes
Servings: 4

Ingredients:
- 1 cup asparagus, chopped
- 1-pound chicken thighs, skinless, boneless
- 1 teaspoon onion powder
- 1 oz scallions, chopped
- 1 tablespoon coconut oil, melted
- 1 teaspoon smoked paprika

Directions:
1. Mix chicken thighs with onion powder, coconut oil, and smoked paprika.
2. Put the chicken thighs in the air fryer and cook at 385F for 20 minutes.
3. Then flip the chicken thighs on another side and top with chopped asparagus and scallions.
4. Cook the meal for 5 minutes more.

Nutrition: calories 257, fat 11.9, fiber 1.1, carbs 2.6, protein 33.8

Nutmeg Chicken Fillets

Prep time: 15 minutes
Cooking time: 12 minutes
Servings:4

Ingredients:
- 16 oz chicken fillets
- 1 teaspoon ground nutmeg
- 1 tablespoon avocado oil
- ½ teaspoon salt

Directions:
1. Mix ground nutmeg with avocado oil and salt.
2. Then rub the chicken fillet with a nutmeg mixture and put it in the air fryer basket.
3. Cook the meal at 385F for 12 minutes.

Nutrition: calories 223, fat 9, fiber 0.3, carbs 0.5, protein 32.9

Chicken Thighs with Kalamata Olives

Preparation time: 10 minutes
Cooking time: 30 minutes
Servings: 4

Ingredients:
- 8 chicken thighs, boneless, skinless
- 1 tablespoon coconut oil, melted
- 1 teaspoon dried basil
- ½ teaspoon cumin seeds
- 4 kalamata olives, sliced

Directions:
1. Rub the chicken thighs with coconut oil, dried basil, and cumin seeds.
2. Put the chicken in the air fryer basket and cook t 375F for 20 minutes.
3. Then flip the chicken thighs on another side, top them with Kalamata olives and cook the meals for 10 minutes more.

Nutrition: calories 590, fat 25.6, fiber 0.2, carbs 0.4, protein 84.6

Taco Chicken

Prep time: 15 minutes
Cooking time: 30 minutes
Servings: 4

Ingredients:
- 1 tablespoon taco seasonings
- 1 tablespoon apple cider vinegar
- 1 tablespoon olive oil
- 2-pounds chicken thighs, skinless, boneless

Directions:

1. Rub the chicken thighs with taco seasonings and sprinkle with olive oil and apple cider vinegar.
2. Put them in the air fryer and cook at 365F for 15 minutes per side.

Nutrition: calories 469, fat 20.3, fiber 0, carbs 1.5, protein 65.6

Spinach Chicken Wings

Preparation time: 10 minutes
Cooking time: 25 minutes
Servings: 4

Ingredients:
- 1 cup fresh spinach, chopped
- 2 tablespoons olive oil
- 1 oz Parmesan, grated
- 1-pound chicken wings, skinless, boneless, chopped

Directions:
1. Brush the air fryer basket with olive oil from inside.
2. Then put the chicken wings inside.
3. Top them with chopped spinach and Parmesan.
4. Cook the meal at 380F for 25 minutes.

Nutrition: calories 214, fat 11.4, fiber 0.2, carbs 0.5, protein 26.5

Keto TSO Chicken

Prep time: 25 minutes
Cooking time: 22 minutes
Servings: 4

Ingredients:
- 1-pound chicken breast, skinless, boneless, chopped
- 1 tablespoon avocado oil
- 1 teaspoon ground black pepper
- 1 teaspoon salt
- 1 tablespoon coconut aminos
- ½ cup almond flour
- 1 teaspoon Erythritol
- 1 chili pepper, chopped
- 2 oz scallions, chopped
- 1 teaspoon coconut oil
- ¼ cup of water

Directions:
1. Rub the chicken with avocado oil, ground black pepper, salt, and coconut aminos/
2. Add water and leave the chicken for 15 minutes to marinate.
3. Meanwhile, mix almond flour with Erythritol, chili pepper, and scallions.
4. Coat the chicken in the almond flour mixture and put it in the air fryer. Add coconut oil.
5. Cook the meal at 375F for 11 minutes per side.

Nutrition: calories 238, fat 11.1, fiber 2.2, carbs 6.7, protein 27.4

Cumin Chicken Thighs

Preparation time: 5 minutes
Cooking time: 25 minutes
Servings: 4

Ingredients:
- 4 chicken thighs, skinless, boneless
- 1 tablespoon coconut oil
- 1 teaspoon ground cumin
- ½ teaspoon salt
- ½ teaspoon smoked paprika

Directions:
1. Mix chicken thighs with coconut oil, cumin, salt, and smoked paprika.
2. Put the chicken thighs in the air fryer basket and cook at 375F for 25 minutes.

Nutrition: calories 309, fat 14.4, fiber 0.2, carbs 0.4, protein 42.4

Cream Cheese Chicken

Prep time: 10 minutes
Cooking time: 25 minutes
Servings: 5

Ingredients:
- 1 ½-pound chicken breast, skinless, boneless
- 1 teaspoon ground paprika
- ½ teaspoon ground turmeric
- 2 teaspoons cream cheese
- 1 oz scallions, chopped
- 1 teaspoon avocado oil
- ½ teaspoon salt

Directions:
1. Rub the chicken breast with ground paprika, turmeric, and salt.
2. Then put the chicken in the air fryer basket.
3. Add avocado oil, scallions, and cream cheese.
4. Cook the meal at 375F for 25 minutes.

Nutrition: calories 165, fat 4.1, fiber 0.4, carbs 0.9, protein 29.1

Jalapeno Chicken Drumsticks

Preparation time: 5 minutes
Cooking time: 25 minutes
Servings: 4

Ingredients:
- 2-pound chicken drumsticks
- 2 jalapeno peppers, minced
- 1 tablespoon avocado oil
- 1 teaspoon ground black pepper
- ½ teaspoon garlic powder

Directions:

1. In the mixing bowl mix chicken drumsticks with jalapeno peppers, avocado oil, ground black pepper, and garlic powder.
2. Put the chicken drumsticks in the air fryer and cook at 370F for 25 minutes.

Nutrition: calories 393, fat 13.5, fiber 0.6, carbs 1.3, protein 62.6

Chicken Quesadilla Melt

Prep time: 15 minutes
Cooking time: 10 minutes
Servings: 2

Ingredients:
- 2 keto tortillas
- 9 oz chicken fillet, cooked, shredded
- 1 jalapeno pepper, sliced
- 3 oz Parmesan, grated
- 1 teaspoon dried dill

Directions:
1. In the mixing bowl, mix shredded chicken with jalapeno pepper, Parmesan, and dried dill.
2. Then spread the mixture over the tortillas and fold them.
3. Put the tortillas in the air fryer basket and cook at 390F for 5 minutes per side.

Nutrition: calories 532, fat 26.6, fiber 4.3, carbs 10.2, Protein 62.8

Provolone Chicken Breasts

Preparation time: 5 minutes
Cooking time: 24 minutes
Servings: 6

Ingredients:
- 3-pounds chicken breast, skinless, boneless

- 1 tablespoon coconut oil
- 5 oz provolone cheese, shredded
- 1 teaspoon dried oregano
- 1 teaspoon dried cilantro

Directions:
1. Rub the chicken breast with dried oregano and cilantro.
2. Then brush the chicken breast with coconut oil and put it in the air fryer basket.
3. Cook it for 20 minutes at 385F.
4. Then top the chicken breast with Provolone cheese and cook the meal for 4 minutes more.

Nutrition: calories 362, fat 14.3, fiber 0.1, carbs 0.7, protein 54.2

Crunchy Turkey Bacon

Prep time: 10 minutes
Cooking time: 8 minutes
Servings: 2

Ingredients:
- 8 oz turkey bacon, sliced
- 1 teaspoon olive oil
- ½ teaspoon liquid stevia

Directions:
1. Sprinkle the turkey bacon with olive oil and liquid stevia and put it in the air fryer basket in one layer.
2. Cook the bacon at 380F for 4 minutes per side.

Nutrition: calories 166, fat 6, fiber 0, carbs 0, protein 22

Cinnamon Chicken Wings

Preparation time: 5 minutes
Cooking time: 30 minutes
Servings: 4

Ingredients:
- 1 tablespoon olive oil
- 2 pounds of chicken wings
- 1 teaspoon ground cinnamon
- ½ teaspoon apple cider vinegar

Directions:
1. Sprinkle the chicken wings with ground cinnamon and apple cider vinegar.
2. Then sprinkle the chicken ings with olive oil and put it in the air fryer.
3. Cook the meal at 375F for 30 minutes. Flip the chicken wings from time to time to avoid burning.

Nutrition: calories 462, fat 20.3, fiber 0.3, carbs 0.5, protein 65.6

Garlic Duck Skin

Prep time: 5 minutes
Cooking time: 6 minutes
Servings: 6

Ingredients:
- 10 oz duck skin
- 1 teaspoon avocado oil
- 1 teaspoon garlic powder

Directions:
1. Mix duck skin with avocado oil and garlic powder.
2. Put it in the air fryer basket and cook for 3 minutes per side at 400F.

Nutrition: calories 196, fat 18.9, fiber 0.1, carbs 0.4, protein 5.6

Coconut Chicken Tenders

Preparation time: 5 minutes
Cooking time: 20 minutes
Servings: 4

Ingredients:

- 2-pounds chicken breast, skinless, boneless
- ½ cup coconut shred
- 2 eggs, beaten
- 1 teaspoon Italian seasonings

Directions:
1. Cut the chicken into tenders and sprinkle with Italian seasonings.
2. Then dip the chicken tenders in the eggs and coat in the coconut shred.
3. Put the chicken tenders in the air fryer basket and cook at 370F for 10 minutes per side.

Nutrition: calories 394, fat 18.2, fiber 2, carbs 4.3, protein 50.9

Pepper Cutlets

Prep time: 10 minutes
Cooking time: 16 minutes
Servings: 4

Ingredients:
- 2-pounds chicken fillet
- 1 teaspoon ground black pepper
- 1 teaspoon coconut oil, melted
- 1 teaspoon chili powder

Directions:
1. Sprinkle the chicken fillets with ground black pepper and chili powder and put in the air fryer basket in one layer.
2. Then sprinkle the chicken with coconut oil and cool at 380F for 8 minutes per side.

Nutrition: calories 444, fat 18.1, fiber 0.4, carbs 0.7, protein 65.8

Sweet and Sour Chicken Drumsticks

Preparation time: 10 minutes
Cooking time: 30 minutes
Servings: 4

Ingredients:
- 1 tablespoon keto tomato paste
- 2 tablespoons avocado oil
- 2 tablespoons coconut aminos
- 1 teaspoon garlic powder
- 1 teaspoon chili flakes
- 2-pounds chicken drumsticks
- 1 teaspoon Erythritol

Directions:
1. Sprinkle the chicken drumsticks with tomato paste, avocado oil, coconut aminos, garlic powder, chili flakes, and Erythritol.
2. Put them in the air fryer and cook at 360F for 15 minutes per side.

Nutrition: calories 401, fat 13.9, fiber 0.6, carbs 2.2, protein 62.8

Apple Cider Vinegar Chicken Thighs

Prep time: 10 minutes
Cooking time: 15 minutes
Servings: 4

Ingredients:
- 16 oz chicken thighs, skinless
- 1 teaspoon chili powder
- 1/3 cup apple cider vinegar
- 1 tablespoon avocado oil

Directions:
1. Sprinkle the chicken thighs with chili powder, apple cider vinegar, and avocado oil.
2. Put them in the air fryer basket and cook at 380F for 15 minutes.

Nutrition: calories 226, fat 9, fiber 0.4, carbs 0.8, protein 32.9

Tarragon Chicken Thighs

Preparation time: 5 minutes
Cooking time: 30 minutes
Servings: 4

Ingredients:
- 2 pounds chicken thighs
- 1 tablespoon dried tarragon
- 1 tablespoon avocado oil
- ½ teaspoon salt

Directions:
1. Mix chicken thighs with dried tarragon, avocado oil, and salt.
2. Put the chicken thighs in the air fryer basket and cook for 15 minutes per side at 360F.

Nutrition: calories 437, fat 17.3, fiber 0.2, carbs 0.4, protein 65.8

Marinara Chicken Wings

Prep time: 10 minutes
Cooking time: 30 minutes
Servings: 5

Ingredients:
- 3-pounds chicken wings
- ¼ cup marinara sauce
- 1 tablespoon coconut oil, melted

Directions:
1. Mix marinara sauce with coconut oil.
2. Then put the chicken wings in the air fryer basket and add marinara sauce mixture.
3. Cook the meal at 360F for 30 minutes.

Nutrition: calories 551, fat 23.2, fiber 0.3, carbs 1.7, protein 79

Lemon Chicken Tenders

Preparation time: 5 minutes
Cooking time: 20 minutes
Servings: 4

Ingredients:
- 2-pounds chicken tenders
- 1 teaspoon lemon zest, grated
- 2 tablespoons lemon juice
- 1 tablespoon avocado oil

Directions:
1. Mix avocado oil with lemon juice and lemon zest.
2. Then mix chicken tenders with lemon mixture and put in the air fryer.
3. Cook the chicken tenders at 365F for 10 minutes per side.

Nutrition: calories 438, fat 17.3, fiber 0.2, carbs 0.5, protein 65.7

Splenda Chicken Wings

Prep time: 15 minutes
Cooking time: 15 minutes
Servings: 8

Ingredients:
- 4-pounds chicken wings
- 1 tablespoon Splenda
- 1 tablespoon avocado oil
- ½ teaspoon ground coriander

Directions:
1. Rub the chicken wings with Splenda, avocado oil, and ground coriander.
2. Put the chicken wings in the air fryer basket and cook at 385F for 15 minutes.

Nutrition: calories 441, fat 17, fiber 0.1, carbs 1.6, protein 65.6

Curry Chicken Wings

Preparation time: 10 minutes
Cooking time: 25 minutes
Servings: 4

Ingredients:
- 2 pounds chicken wings, boneless
- 1 teaspoon curry powder
- 3 tablespoons heavy cream
- 1 tablespoon avocado oil

Directions:
1. Mix heavy cream with curry powder.
2. Then mix chicken wings with curry mixture and put in the air fryer.
3. Sprinkle the chicken wings with avocado oil and cook them for 25 minutes at 375F.

Nutrition: calories 476, fat 21.5, fiber 0.3, carbs 0.8, protein 65.9

Thyme Chicken Drumsticks

Prep time: 10 minutes
Cooking time: 21 minutes
Servings: 4

Ingredients:
- 2-pounds chicken drumsticks
- 1 tablespoon dried thyme
- 1 tablespoon coconut oil, melted
- 1 teaspoon salt

Directions:
1. Mix chicken drumsticks with dried thyme, coconut oil, and salt.
2. Put the chicken drumsticks in the air fryer basket and cook at 385F for 21 minutes.

Nutrition: calories 414, fat 16.4, fiber 0.3, carbs 0.4, protein 62.4

Sage Turkey Breast

Preparation time: 10 minutes
Cooking time: 25 minutes
Servings: 4

Ingredients:
- 2-pounds turkey breast, skinless, boneless
- 1 tablespoon dried sage
- 1 teaspoon salt
- 2 tablespoons avocado oil

Directions:
1. Put the turkey breast in the air fryer basket and sprinkle with dried sage, salt, and avocado oil.
2. Cook it at 385F for 12 minutes per side.
3. Then cook the turkey breast for 1 minute more at 400F.

Nutrition: calories 247, fat 14.7, fiber 1.6, carbs 10.2, protein 38.9

Scallions Chicken Tenders

Prep time: 15 minutes
Cooking time: 10 minutes
Servings: 2

Ingredients:
- 8 oz chicken fillet
- 2 oz scallions, chopped
- 2 tablespoons olive oil
- 1 teaspoon salt
- ½ teaspoon ground black pepper

Directions:
1. Cut the chicken into the tenders and sprinkle with olive oil, salt, and ground black pepper.
2. Put the chicken tenders in the air fryer basket in one layer and cook at 390F for 4 minutes per side.

3. Then top the chicken tenders with scallions and cook it for 2 minutes more.

Nutrition: calories 346, fat 22.5, fiber 0.9, carbs 2.4, protein 33.4

Turkey Spread

Preparation time: 5 minutes
Cooking time: 24 minutes
Servings: 4

Ingredients:
- 3 tablespoons butter
- 1-pound ground turkey
- 1 teaspoon olive oil
- 1 teaspoon ground black pepper
- ½ teaspoon dried rosemary

Directions:
1. In the mixing bowl, mix butter with ground turkey, olive oil, ground black pepper, and dried rosemary.
2. Put the mixture in the air fryer and cook it for 24 minutes at 355F. Stir the mixture from time to time to avoid burning.
3. Blend the cooked turkey mixture and put it in the serving bowl.

Nutrition: calories 309, fat 22.3, fiber 0.2, carbs 0.5, protein 31.2

Spicy Chicken Roll

Prep time: 15 minutes
Cooking time: 25 minutes
Servings:5

Ingredients:
- 1-pound chicken fillet
- 1 teaspoon cayenne pepper
- 1 oz scallions, chopped
- 1 oz Parmesan, grated
- ½ teaspoon dried basil
- ½ teaspoon olive oil
- ½ teaspoon chili powder

Directions:
1. Beat the chicken fillet with the help of the kitchen hammer to get the flat cutlet.
2. Then rub it with cayenne pepper, dried basil, olive oil, and chili powder.
3. Top the chicken fillet with Parmesan and scallions and roll into a roll.
4. Put it in the air fryer basket and cook it for 25 minutes at 385F.

Nutrition: calories 198, fat 8.5, fiber 0.3, carbs 1, protein 28.2

Turkey in Sweet Sauce

Preparation time: 10 minutes
Cooking time: 30 minutes
Servings: 4

Ingredients:
- 1-pound turkey breast, skinless, boneless, chopped
- 1 tablespoon coconut oil
- 1 tablespoon Erythritol
- 1 jalapeno pepper, chopped
- 1 teaspoon ground paprika

Directions:
1. Grease the air fryer basket with coconut oil.
2. Rub the turkey breast with Erythritol and ground paprika. Put the turkey breast in the air fryer and add jalapeno pepper.
3. Cook the meal at 365F for 30 minutes. Flip the turkey after 15 minutes of cooking.
4. Slice the turkey breast and sprinkle it with sweet liquid (sauce) from the air fryer basket.

Nutrition: calories 150, fat 5.4, fiber 0.9, carbs 5.3, protein 19.5

Wrapped Chicken

Prep time: 15 minutes
Cooking time: 25 minutes
Servings: 2

Ingredients:
- 4 chicken drumsticks
- 4 bacon slices
- 1 teaspoon ground nutmeg
- ¼ teaspoon salt

Directions:
1. Rub the chicken drumsticks with ground nutmeg and salt.
2. Then wrap the chicken in bacon slices and put in the air fryer.
3. Cook the meal at 375F for 25 minutes.

Nutrition: calories 367, fat 21.5, fiber 0.2, carbs 1.1, protein 39.4

Mustard Chicken Cubes

Preparation time: 5 minutes
Cooking time: 20 minutes
Servings: 4

Ingredients:
- 16 oz chicken breast, skinless, boneless, cubed
- 1 tablespoon avocado oil
- 1 teaspoon mustard
- 1 teaspoon cream cheese

Directions:
1. In the mixing bowl, mix avocado oil with mustard and cream cheese.
2. When the mixture is smooth, add chicken cubes and mix well.

3. Transfer the chicken cubes in the air fryer basket and cook at 360F for 20 minutes.

Nutrition: calories 141, fat 3.8, fiber 0.3, carbs 0.5, protein 24.4

Chicken Pate

Prep time: 15 minutes
Cooking time: 10 minutes
Servings: 6

Ingredients:
- ½ cup coconut oil, softened
- 2-pounds chicken fillet
- 1 tablespoon avocado oil
- 1 teaspoon onion powder
- 1 teaspoon salt

Directions:
1. Mix chicken fillet with avocado oil and put it in the air fryer.
2. Cook it at 395F for 10 minutes.
3. Then chop the chicken and put it in the blender.
4. Add remaining ingredients and blend until smooth.

Nutrition: calories 448, fat 29.7, fiber 0.1, carbs 0.5, protein 43.8

Turkey Spread

Preparation time: 5 minutes
Cooking time: 30 minutes
Servings: 4

Ingredients:
- 1-pound turkey breast, skinless, boneless, chopped
- 1 tablespoon coconut oil
- 3 tablespoons cream cheese
- 1 teaspoon cayenne pepper
- ½ teaspoon dried oregano
- 1 teaspoon salt

Directions:
1. Mix turkey breast with cayenne pepper, dried oregano, and salt.
2. Put it in the air fryer and cook at 350F for 15 minutes per side.
3. Then transfer the cooked turkey in the blender and blend until smooth.
4. Mix the blended turkey with remaining ingredients and transfer it in the serving bowl.

Nutrition: calories 175, fat 8, fiber 0.8, carbs 5.3, protein 20

Tomato Chicken Drumsticks

Prep time: 15 minutes + 8 hours for marinating
Cooking time: 18 minutes
Servings: 8

Ingredients:
• 8 chicken drumsticks
• 1 tablespoon tomato paste
• 1 teaspoon cayenne pepper
• 2 tablespoons apple cider vinegar
• 1 tablespoon avocado oil

Directions:
1. Mix tomato paste with cayenne pepper, apple cider vinegar, and avocado oil.
2. Then rub the chicken drumsticks with the tomato paste mixture and marinate for 8 hours.
3. Put the chicken drumsticks in the air fryer and cook at 360F for 18 minutes.

Nutrition: calories 83, fat 2.9, fiber 0.2, carbs 0.6, protein 12.8

Turkey Leg

Preparation time: 10 minutes

Cooking time: 40 minutes
Servings: 4

Ingredients:
• 2-pounds turkey leg
• ¼ cup marinara sauce
• 1 teaspoon ground nutmeg
• 1 tablespoon coconut oil, melted
• ½ teaspoon dried thyme

Directions:
1. Mix the turkey leg with all remaining ingredients and put it in the air fryer.
2. Cook it at 355F for 40 minutes. Flip it from time to time to avoid burning.

Nutrition: calories 518, fat 26.3, fiber 0.6, carbs 2.5, protein 63.5

Tender Chicken Meatballs

Prep time: 20 minutes
Cooking time: 11 minutes
Servings: 6

Ingredients:
• 3-pounds ground chicken
• 1 teaspoon cream cheese
• 1 teaspoon dried cilantro
• 1 teaspoon garlic powder
• Cooking spray

Directions:
1. Mix the ground chicken with cream cheese, dried cilantro, and garlic powder.
2. Make the meatballs from the chicken mixture and put them in the air fryer basket.
3. Cook the meatballs at 360F for 11 minutes.

Nutrition: calories 434, fat 17, fiber 0.1, carbs 0.4, protein 65.7

Scallions Meatballs

Preparation time: 15 minutes
Cooking time: 24 minutes
Servings: 2

Ingredients:
- 2 cups ground chicken
- 2 oz scallions, minced
- ½ teaspoon ground black pepper
- 1 teaspoon coconut cream
- ½ teaspoon salt
- 1 teaspoon olive oil

Directions:
1. Mix ground chicken with minced scallions, ground black pepper, coconut cream, and salt.
2. Make the meatballs and put them in the air fryer.
3. Sprinkle the meatballs with olive oil and cook at 360F for 12 minutes per side.

Nutrition: calories 302, fat 13.4, fiber 0.9, carbs 2.6, protein 41.1

Dill Chicken Fillets

Prep time: 15 minutes
Cooking time: 14 minutes
Servings: 2

Ingredients:
- 12 oz chicken fillets
- 1 tablespoon dried dill
- 1 tablespoon avocado oil

Directions:
1. Cut the chicken fillet into servings and sprinkle with dried dill and avocado oil.
2. Put the chicken fillets in the air fryer basket and cook at 360F for 7 minutes per side.

Nutrition: calories 336, fat 13.6, fiber 0.5, carbs 1.3, protein 49.6

Sweet Chicken Strips

Preparation time: 10 minutes
Cooking time: 30 minutes
Servings: 4

Ingredients:
- 2-pound chicken fillet, cut into strips
- 1 tablespoon Erythritol
- ¼ cup heavy cream
- ½ teaspoon white pepper
- Cooking spray

Directions:
1. Mix the chicken strips with Erythritol, heavy cream, and white pepper.
2. Spray the air fryer basket with cooking spray and put the chicken strips inside.
3. Cook the chicken strips at 350F for 30 minutes.

Nutrition: calories 457, fat 19.6, fiber 0.1, carbs 0.4, protein 65.8

Mint Chicken Sausages

Prep time: 20 minutes
Cooking time: 10 minutes
Servings: 5

Ingredients:
- 2-pound chicken sausages
- 1 tablespoon olive oil
- 1 teaspoon dried mint
- ¼ teaspoon salt

Directions:
1. Sprinkle the chicken sausages with dried mint and salt.

2. Then put the chicken sausages in the air fryer and sprinkle with olive oil.
3. Cook the meal at 390F for 5 minutes per side.

Nutrition: calories 326, fat 20.4, fiber 1, carbs 10.7, protein 20.8

Turkey Cups

Preparation time: 5 minutes
Cooking time: 25 minutes
Servings: 4

Ingredients:
- 17 oz ground turkey
- ¼ cup cream cheese
- 1 teaspoon Italian seasonings
- 1 teaspoon coconut oil

Directions:
1. Grease the ramekins with coconut oil.
2. Then mix ground turkey with cream cheese and Italian seasonings.
3. Put the ground turkey mixture in the ramekins and cook in the air fryer at 375F for 25 minutes.

Nutrition: calories 299, fat 19.8, fiber 0, carbs 0.5, protein 34.1

Egg Strips

Prep time: 15 minutes
Cooking time: 14 minutes
Servings: 6

Ingredients:
- 2-pound chicken breast, skinless, boneless
- 4 eggs, beaten
- ½ cup coconut flour
- 1 teaspoon Italian seasonings

Directions:

1. Cut the chicken breast into the strips and sprinkle with Italian seasonings.
2. Then dip the chicken strips in the egg and coat in the coconut flour.
3. Cook the chicken strips in the air fryer at 375F for 7 minutes per side.

Nutrition: calories 217, fat 7.9, fiber 4, carbs 7, protein 37.4

Celery Chicken Breast

Preparation time: 5 minutes
Cooking time: 30 minutes
Servings: 4

Ingredients:
- 1 teaspoon onion powder
- 1 teaspoon garlic powder
- 2-pounds chicken breast, skinless, boneless
- 2 tablespoons ground celery root
- 1 tablespoon avocado oil

Directions:
1. In the shallow bowl, mix onion powder with garlic powder, and ground celery root.
2. Mix the chicken breast with the spice mixture and sprinkle with avocado oil.
3. Cook the chicken breast at 360f for 15 minutes per side.

Nutrition: calories 268, fat 6.1, fiber 0.3, carbs 1.2, protein 48.3

Turkey Pockets

Prep time: 15 minutes
Cooking time: 4 minutes
Servings: 4

Ingredients:
- 4 keto tortillas

- 1 bell pepper, chopped
- 3 oz Provolone cheese, grated
- 1 teaspoon dried parsley
- 1-pound turkey breast, boiled, chopped

Directions:
1. Mix the bell pepper with cheese, dried parsley, and turkey breast.
2. Then top the tortillas with turkey mixture and fold in the shape of pockets.
3. Cook the turkey pockets at 400F for 4 minutes.

Nutrition: calories 352, fat 15.6, fiber 5, carbs 15.5, protein 37.1

Stuffed Turkey

Preparation time: 15 minutes
Cooking time: 30 minutes
Servings: 4

Ingredients:
- 2-pound turkey fillet
- 1 cup mushrooms, chopped
- 1 teaspoon garlic powder
- 2 oz scallions, chopped
- 1 tablespoon coconut oil
- 1 teaspoon olive oil
- 1 teaspoon chili powder

Directions:
1. Mix chili powder with mushrooms, garlic powder, olive oil, and scallions.
2. Then make the cut in the shape of pocket in the turkey fillet. Fill it with mushroom mixture and secure the cut with the help of the toothpick.
3. Grease the air fryer basket with coconut oil and put the stuffed turkey inside.
4. Cook it at 380f for 30 minutes.

Nutrition: calories 266, fat 5.8, fiber 0.8, carbs 2.5, protein 48.1

Cajun Chicken

Prep time: 15 minutes
Cooking time: 20 minutes
Servings: 3

Ingredients:
- 1.5-pound chicken thighs, skinless, boneless
- 1 tablespoon Cajun seasonings
- 1 tablespoon coconut oil, melted

Directions:
1. Mix chicken thighs with Cajun seasonings.
2. Put them in the air fryer basket. Add coconut oil.
3. Cook the meal at 375F for 10 minutes per side.

Nutrition: calories 470, fat 21.3, fiber 0, carbs 0, protein 65.7

Ginger Turkey

Preparation time: 5 minutes
Cooking time: 15 minutes
Servings: 4

Ingredients:
- 2-pound turkey breast, skinless, boneless, chopped
- 1 tablespoon ginger powder
- ½ teaspoon salt
- 1 tablespoon olive oil

Directions:
1. Mix turkey breast with ginger powder, salt, and olive oil.
2. Cook the turkey at 385F for 15 minutes.

Nutrition: calories 271, fat 7.3, fiber 1.3, carbs 10.5, protein 38.8

Sweet Paprika Chicken Breast

Prep time: 10 minutes
Cooking time: 30 minutes
Servings: 3

Ingredients:
- 1-pound chicken breast, skinless, boneless
- 1 tablespoon ground paprika
- 1 teaspoon salt
- 1 teaspoon ground turmeric
- 1 tablespoon avocado oil

Directions:
1. Rub the chicken with all remaining ingredients and put in the air fryer basket.
2. Cook the chicken breast at 360F for 30 minutes.

Nutrition: calories 188, fat 4.7, fiber 1.2, carbs 2, protein 32.5

Turkey Mash

Preparation time: 5 minutes
Cooking time: 35 minutes
Servings: 4

Ingredients:
- 1-pound turkey breast, skinless, boneless, chopped
- 2 tablespoons mascarpone
- 1 teaspoon garlic powder
- 1 tablespoon dried parsley
- Cooking spray

Directions:
1. Spray the air fryer basket with cooking spray from inside.

2. Then put all remaining ingredients in the air fryer basket and carefully mix.
3. Cook the turkey mash at 355F for 35 minutes.

Nutrition: calories 134, fat 2.9, fiber 0.7, carbs 5.6, protein 20.4

Marinated Basil Chicken Breast

Prep time: 25 minutes
Cooking time: 30 minutes
Servings: 5

Ingredients:
- 2-pounds chicken breast, skinless, boneless, chopped
- 2 teaspoons dried basil
- 3 tablespoons apple cider vinegar
- 2 tablespoons avocado oil
- 1 teaspoon salt
- 1 teaspoon ground black pepper

Directions:
1. Mix chicken breast with dried basil, apple cider vinegar, avocado oil, salt, and ground black pepper.
2. Then leave the chicken for 20 minutes to marinate.
3. Put the marinated chicken in the air fryer and cook for 30 minutes at 370F.

Nutrition: calories 217, fat 5.3, fiber 0.4, carbs 0.7, protein 38.6

Ground Chicken Bowl

Preparation time: 10 minutes
Cooking time: 35 minutes
Servings: 4

Ingredients:
- 1-pound ground chicken
- 2 cups green beans, chopped

- 1 cup chicken broth
- 1 teaspoon Italian seasonings
- 1 teaspoon salt
- 1 cup Cheddar cheese, shredded
- 1 teaspoon avocado oil

Directions:
1. Mix ground chicken with Italian seasonings, salt, and avocado oil.
2. Put the mixture in the air fryer basket.
3. Add chicken broth, green beans, and cheddar cheese.
4. Cook the meal at 365F for 35 minutes.

Nutrition: calories 361, fat 18.7, fiber 1.9, carbs 4.7, protein 42.1

Mozzarella Chicken Fillets

Prep time: 15 minutes
Cooking time: 30 minutes
Servings: 4

Ingredients:
- 1 cup Mozzarella, shredded
- 1 teaspoon dried basil
- 1 teaspoon coconut oil
- 1 teaspoon ground black pepper
- 2-pounds chicken breast, skinless, boneless, sliced

Directions:
1. Grease the air fryer basket with coconut oil.
2. Then mix chicken breast with ground black pepper and dried basil.
3. Put it in the air fryer basket and flatten gently.
4. Then top the chicken breast with Mozzarella and cook the meal at 365F for 30 minutes.

Nutrition: calories 290, fat 8.1, fiber 0.1, carbs 0.6, protein 50.2

Chicken Pan

Preparation time: 10 minutes
Cooking time: 35 minutes
Servings: 4

Ingredients:
- 1 cup white cabbage, shredded
- 1-pound chicken fillet, chopped
- 1 teaspoon chili powder
- 1 teaspoon dried cilantro
- 1 tablespoon coconut oil, melted
- ½ teaspoon salt
- ½ cup heavy cream

Directions:
1. Put all ingredients in the air fryer basket and carefully mix the mixture.
2. Cook the meal at 360F for 35 minutes.

Nutrition: calories 303, fat 17.5, fiber 0.7, carbs 1.8, protein 33.4

Cayenne Pepper Chicken Halves

Prep time: 10 minutes
Cooking time: 30 minutes
Servings: 4

Ingredients:
- 2-pounds chicken, halved
- 1 tablespoon cayenne pepper
- 1 tablespoon apple cider vinegar
- 1 tablespoon avocado oil

Directions:
1. Rub the chicken halves with cayenne pepper, apple cider vinegar, and avocado oil.
2. Put the chicken halves in the air fryer and cook them at 360F for 30 minutes per side.

Nutrition: calories 352, fat 7.5, fiber 0.5, carbs 1, protein 65.9

Beef and Lamb

Ginger Lamb

Prep time: 10 minutes
Cooking time: 30 minutes
Servings: 2

Ingredients:
- 15 oz lamb sirloin
- 1 tablespoon avocado oil
- 1 teaspoon ginger powder
- ½ teaspoon onion powder
- 1 teaspoon keto tomato paste

Directions:
1. Rub the lamb sirloin with ginger powder and onion powder.
2. Then mix avocado oil with tomato paste.
3. Brush the lamb sirloin with tomato mixture and put it in the air fryer basket.
4. Cook the meal at 360F for 30 minutes.

Nutrition: calories 450, fat 20.5, fiber 0.6, carbs 2, protein 60.6

Garlic Meatballs

Prep time: 20 minutes
Cooking time: 10 minutes
Servings: 4

Ingredients:
- 2 cups ground beef
- 1 tablespoon garlic powder
- 1 teaspoon chili powder
- 1 teaspoon dried cilantro
- 1 tablespoon almond flour
- Cooking spray

Directions:

1. In the mixing bowl, mix ground beef with garlic powder, chili powder, dried cilantro, and almond flour.
2. Make the meatballs and put them in the air fryer basket.
3. Spray the meatballs with cooking spray and cook at 400F for 5 minutes per side.

Nutrition: calories 118, fat 7, fiber 0.6, carbs 2.3, protein 11.3

Parmesan Beef Meatballs

Prep time: 15 minutes
Cooking time: 8 minutes
Servings: 6

Ingredients:
- 2-pounds ground beef
- 1 tablespoon taco seasonings
- 2 oz Parmesan, grated
- 1 teaspoon olive oil

Directions:
1. Brush the air fryer basket with olive oil.
2. Then mix all remaining ingredients and make the meatballs.
3. Put the meatballs in the air fryer basket and cook them at 390F for 4 minutes per side.

Nutrition: calories 323, fat 12.2, fiber 0, carbs 1.3, protein 48.9

Beef and Greens Bowl

Preparation time: 5 minutes
Cooking time: 45 minutes
Servings: 4

Ingredients:
- 1-pound beef sirloin, chopped
- 2 cups fresh spinach, chopped
- 1 cup heavy cream
- 1 teaspoon Italian seasonings
- 1 teaspoon avocado oil
- 1 teaspoon ground turmeric

Directions:
1. Mix all ingredients in the mixing bowl.
2. Then transfer the beef sirloin mixture in the air fryer basket.
3. Cook the meat at 350F for 45 minutes.

Nutrition: calories 325, fat 18.8, fiber 0.5, carbs 1.9, protein 35.5

Eggplant and Beef Sauté

Preparation time: 5 minutes
Cooking time: 45 minutes
Servings: 4

Ingredients:
- 1-pound beef sirloin, chopped
- 1 eggplant, chopped
- 1 teaspoon salt
- 1 teaspoon ground black pepper
- 1 teaspoon dried cilantro
- 1 cup beef broth

Directions:
1. Put all ingredients in the air fryer basket and carefully mix.
2. Cook the saute at 360F for 45 minutes.

Nutrition: calories 250, fat 7.6, fiber 4.2, carbs 7.3, protein 36.8

Beef Popcorn

Preparation time: 10 minutes
Cooking time: 25 minutes

Servings: 4

Ingredients:
- 2-pounds beef sirloin, cubed
- 2 eggs, beaten
- 3 tablespoons almond flour
- 1 teaspoon chili powder
- ½ teaspoon ground turmeric
- 1 teaspoon avocado oil

Directions:
1. Mix beef sirloins with eggs, almond flour, chili powder, and ground turmeric.
2. Then transfer the meat cubes in the air fryer and sprinkle with avocado oil.
3. Cook the beef popcorn at 375F for 25 minutes. Shake the meal every 5 minutes.

Nutrition: calories 487, fat 19.2, fiber 0.9, carbs 1.9, protein 72.8

Tender Meat Salad

Preparation time: 10 minutes
Cooking time: 25 minutes
Servings: 4

Ingredients:
- 1-pound beef sirloin, sliced
- 1 teaspoon white pepper
- ½ teaspoon salt
- 1 teaspoon coconut oil, melted
- 1 cup lettuce, chopped
- 2 pecans, chopped
- 1 tablespoon avocado oil

Directions:
1. In the mixing bowl, mix beef sirloin with white pepper, salt, and coconut oil.
2. Put the beef in the air fryer basket and cook at 365F for 25 minutes.

3. Then mix beef sirloin with lettuce, pecans, and avocado oil.
4. Shake the salad gently.

Nutrition: calories 277, fat 13.7, fiber 1.1, carbs 2, protein 35.3

Coconut Beef

Preparation time: 10 minutes
Cooking time: 35 minutes
Servings: 2

Ingredients:
- 16 oz beef sirloin, sliced
- ½ cup coconut cream
- 1 teaspoon ground paprika
- ½ teaspoon ground black pepper
- ½ teaspoon olive oil

Directions:
1. Mix beef sirloin with ground paprika, ground black pepper, and olive oil.
2. Transfer the mixture in the air fryer basket and add coconut cream.
3. Cook the coconut beef at 365F for 35 minutes.

Nutrition: calories 574, fat 29.8, fiber 1.9, carbs 4.3, protein 70.4

Baked Beef Bowl

Preparation time: 10 minutes
Cooking time: 50 minutes
Servings: 2

Ingredients:
- 1-pound beef sirloin, chopped
- 1 teaspoon ground nutmeg
- 1 teaspoon salt
- 1 cup radish, chopped
- 1 tablespoon avocado oil
- ½ teaspoon dried basil

- ¼ cup of water

Directions:
1. Put all ingredients in the air fryer basket and carefully mix.
2. Cook the beef meal at 355F for 50 minutes.

Nutrition: calories 446, fat 15.5, fiber 1.5, carbs 2.9, protein 69.4

Beef Roast

Preparation time: 5 minutes
Cooking time: 30 minutes
Servings: 4

Ingredients:
- 2-pounds beef roast, roughly chopped
- 1 teaspoon ground black pepper
- 1 teaspoon minced garlic
- 2 tablespoons avocado oil
- 1 teaspoon dried oregano
- ½ teaspoon cayenne pepper

Directions:
1. Rub the beef roast with ground black pepper, minced garlic, avocado oil, dried oregano, and cayenne pepper.
2. Put the beef in the air fryer basket and cook at 365F for 30 minutes.

Nutrition: calories 435, fat 15.1, fiber 0.7, carbs 1.3, protein 69.1

Fast Mongolian Beef

Prep time: 15 minutes
Cooking time: 20 minutes
Servings: 2

Ingredients:
- 10 oz beef steak, chopped

- 2 tablespoons almond flour
- 1 teaspoon avocado oil
- ½ teaspoon onion powder
- 4 tablespoons coconut aminos
- 1 teaspoon Erythritol

Directions:
1. Mix the beef steak with onion powder, coconut aminos, and Erythritol.
2. Then coat every beef steak piece with almond flour and put in the air fryer basket.
3. Sprinkle the beef with avocado oil and cook at 365F for 10 minutes per side.

Nutrition: calories 341, fat 12.5, fiber 0.9, carbs 10.6, protein 44.6

Beef Under Cabbage Blanket

Preparation time: 10 minutes
Cooking time: 50 minutes
Servings: 4

Ingredients:
- 2-pounds beef sirloin, diced
- 1 cup white cabbage, shredded
- ½ cup beef broth
- 1 teaspoon taco seasonings
- 1 teaspoon coconut oil
- 1 teaspoon salt

Directions:
1. Mix beef sirloin with taco seasonings and salt.
2. Put the coconut oil in the air fryer basket. Add beef sirloin and beef broth.
3. Then top the beef with white cabbage.
4. Cook the meal at 360F for 50 minutes.

Nutrition: calories 440, fat 15.5, fiber 0.4, carbs 1.1, protein 69.6

Coconut Beef Steak

Prep time: 10 minutes
Cooking time: 16 minutes
Servings: 4

Ingredients:
- 2-pounds beef steak
- 3 tablespoons coconut oil
- 1 teaspoon coconut shred
- 1 teaspoon dried basil

Directions:
1. Rub the beef steak with coconut shred and dried basil.
2. Then brush the beef steak with coconut oil and put it in the air fryer.
3. Cook the beef steak at 390F for 8 minutes per side.

Nutrition: calories 509, fat 24.3, fiber 0, carbs 0, protein 68.8

Beef Bread

Preparation time: 10 minutes
Cooking time: 25 minutes
Servings: 4

Ingredients:
- 2-pounds ground beef
- 1 teaspoon minced garlic
- 1 tablespoon dried parsley
- 1 teaspoon ground turmeric
- ¼ cup coconut flour
- 1 tablespoon coconut oil, softened

Directions:
1. In the mixing bowl mix ground beef with minced garlic, dried parsley, ground turmeric, and coconut flour.

2. After this, grease the air fryer basket with coconut oil from inside.
3. Put the ground beef mixture in the air fryer basket and flatten gently.
4. Cook the beef bread at 370F for 25 minutes.

Nutrition: calories 484, fat 18.3, fiber 3.2, carbs 5.7, protein 69.9

Onion Beef Bites

Prep time: 10 minutes
Cooking time: 30 minutes
Servings: 4

Ingredients:
• 2-pound beef fillet
• 1 tablespoon onion powder
• ¼ cup heavy cream
• ½ teaspoon salt
• 1 teaspoon olive oil

Directions:
1. Cut the beef fillet into bites and sprinkle with onion powder and salt.
2. Then put the beef bites in the air fryer and add heavy cream.
3. Cook the beef bites at 360F for 15 minutes per side.

Nutrition: calories 295, fat 14.1, fiber 0.1, carbs 5.7, protein 36.8

Italian Style Beef

Preparation time: 10 minutes
Cooking time: 35 minutes
Servings: 4

Ingredients:
• 2-pounds beef steak, cut into strips
• ¼ cup plain yogurt
• 1 teaspoon lemon juice
• 1 teaspoon white pepper

• ½ teaspoon dried oregano
• Cooking spray

Directions:
1. Mix plain yogurt with lemon juice, white pepper, and dried oregano.
2. Then put beef strips in the plain yogurt mixture.
3. Spray the air fryer basket with cooking spray.
4. Put the beef strips mixture in the air fryer and cook them for 35 minutes at 360F.

Nutrition: calories 434, fat 14.4, fiber 0.2, carbs 1.6, protein 69.8

BBQ Beef

Prep time: 15 minutes
Cooking time: 15 minutes
Servings: 4

Ingredients:
• 4 beef steaks
• 1 cup keto BBQ sauce
• 1 tablespoon olive oil

Directions:
1. Mix olive oil with BBQ sauce.
2. Then mix beef steaks with sauce mixture and put in the air fryer.
3. Cook the beef at 400F for 15 minutes.

Nutrition: calories 603, fat 25.3, fiber 0.4, carbs 2.7, protein 66.2

Minced Beef Bowl

Preparation time: 5 minutes
Cooking time: 30 minutes
Servings: 4

Ingredients:

- 1 cup bell pepper, diced
- 1-pound ground beef
- 1 garlic clove, diced
- 1 teaspoon dried oregano
- 1 teaspoon coconut oil
- 1 tablespoon cream cheese

Directions:
1. Mix all ingredients from the list above in the mixing bowl.
2. Then transfer the mixture in the air fryer basket and cook at 365F for 30 minutes.

Nutrition: calories 241, fat 9.2, fiber 0.6, carbs 2.8, protein 35

Stuffed Beef Roll

Prep time: 20 minutes
Cooking time: 40 minutes
Servings: 4

Ingredients:
- 1-pound beef loin
- 2 oz mushrooms, chopped
- 1 teaspoon onion powder
- 1 oz bacon, chopped, cooked
- ½ teaspoon dried dill
- 1 teaspoon chili powder
- 1 tablespoon avocado oil
- ½ teaspoon cream cheese

Directions:
1. Beat the beef loin with the help of the kitchen hammer to get the flat loin.
2. After this, mix mushrooms with onion powder, bacon, dried dill, chili powder, and cream cheese.
3. Put the mixture over the beef loin and roll it.
4. Secure the beef roll with toothpicks and brush with avocado oil.
5. Cook the beef roll at 370F for 40 minutes.

Nutrition: calories 258, fat 13.2, fiber 0.6, carbs 1.7, protein 33.7

Garlic Beef Steak

Preparation time: 10 minutes
Cooking time: 14 minutes
Servings: 4

Ingredients:
- 4 beef steaks
- 1 teaspoon garlic powder
- 1 tablespoon coconut oil

Directions:
1. Mix beef steaks with garlic powder and coconut oil.
2. Put the beef steaks in the air fryer and cook them for 7 minutes per side at 400F.

Nutrition: calories 190, fat 8.7, fiber 0.1, carbs 0.5, protein 25.9

Za'atar Beef Chops

Prep time: 10 minutes
Cooking time: 11 minutes
Servings: 6

Ingredients:
- 6 beef chops
- 1 tablespoon coconut oil, melted
- 1 tablespoon za'atar seasonings

Directions:
1. Mix za'atar seasonings with coconut oil.
2. Brush the beef chops with coconut oil mixture and put it in the air fryer.
3. Cook the meal at 400F for 11 minutes.

Nutrition: calories 57, fat 3.5, fiber 0, carbs 0.5, protein 5.7

Tomato Rib Eye Steaks

Preparation time: 10 minutes
Cooking time: 24 minutes
Servings: 4

Ingredients:
* 3-pound rib-eye steak
* 1 tablespoon keto tomato paste
* 1 tablespoon avocado oil
* 1 teaspoon salt
* 1 teaspoon cayenne pepper

Directions:
1. In the shallow bowl, mix tomato paste with avocado oil, salt, and cayenne pepper.
2. Then run the beef with tomato mixture and put it in the air fryer.
3. Cook the meal at 380F for 12 minutes per side.

Nutrition: calories 943, fat 75.8, fiber 0.4, carbs 1.2, protein 60.5

Mustard Beef Loin

Prep time: 10 minutes
Cooking time: 40 minutes
Servings: 7

Ingredients:
* 4-pounds beef loin
* 2 tablespoon Dijon mustard
* 1 tablespoon olive oil
* ½ tablespoon apple cider vinegar

Directions:
1. Mix mustard with olive oil and apple cider vinegar.

2. Then rub the beef loin with mustard mixture and put it in the air fryer.
3. Cook the meal at 375F for 20 minutes per side.

Nutrition: calories 492, fat 23.8, fiber 0.2, carbs 0.3, protein 69.5

Curry Beef

Preparation time: 15 minutes
Cooking time: 30 minutes
Servings: 4

Ingredients:
* 2-pounds beef tenderloin, chopped
* ¼ cup heavy cream
* 1 teaspoon curry paste
* ¼ teaspoon minced garlic
* 1 teaspoon coconut oil, melted

Directions:
1. Mix heavy cream with curry paste and minced garlic.
2. Then put the beef tenderloin in the curry mixture and leave for 10 minutes to marinate.
3. Put the coconut oil in the air fryer.
4. Add curry mixture and cook at 370F for 30 minutes.

Nutrition: calories 511, fat 25.4, fiber 0, carbs 0.6, protein 65.9

Rosemary Beef Meatballs

Preparation time: 5 minutes
Cooking time: 25 minutes
Servings: 4

Ingredients:
* 2-pound ground beef
* 1 teaspoon dried rosemary
* 1 teaspoon onion powder

- ½ teaspoon salt
- 1 tablespoon olive oil

Directions:
1. Mix ground beef with dried rosemary, onion powder, and salt.
2. Make the meatballs and put them in the air fryer.
3. Sprinkle the meatballs with olive oil and cook at 360F for 25 minutes.

Nutrition: calories 454, fat 17.7, fiber 0.2, carbs 0.7, protein 68.9

Basil Beef

Preparation time: 10 minutes
Cooking time: 40 minutes
Servings: 4

Ingredients:
- 3-pounds beef steak
- 2 tablespoons coconut oil, melted
- 1 tablespoon dried basil
- ½ teaspoon salt

Directions:
1. Rub the beef steak with dried basil and salt.
2. Then put the steak in the air fryer and sprinkle with coconut oil.
3. Cook the beef at 365F for 20 minutes per side.

Nutrition: calories 691, fat 28, fiber 0, carbs 0, protein 103.2

Beef Casserole

Preparation time: 10 minutes
Cooking time: 40 minutes
Servings: 4

Ingredients:
- 2 oz Provolone cheese, grated

- 1 teaspoon coconut oil, softened
- 1 teaspoon dried cilantro
- 2-pounds ground beef
- 1 jalapeno pepper, sliced
- 1 teaspoon chili powder
- ¼ cup beef broth

Directions:
1. Grease the air fryer basket with coconut oil.
2. Then mix ground beef with dried cilantro, jalapeno pepper, and chili powder.
3. Put the mixture in the air fryer basket.
4. Add beef broth and Provolone cheese.
5. Cook the casserole at 360F for 40 minutes.

Nutrition: calories 486, fat 19.3, fiber 0.3, carbs 0.9, protein 72.9

Garlic Burgers

Prep time: 15 minutes
Cooking time: 15 minutes
Servings: 4

Ingredients:
- 2-pounds ground beef
- 1 teaspoon garlic powder
- 1 egg, beaten
- 1 teaspoon ground black pepper

Directions:
1. Mix ground beef with garlic powder, ground black pepper, and egg.
2. Make the burgers from the mixture and put them in the air fryer in one layer.
3. Cook the burgers at 385F for 15 minutes.

Nutrition: calories 441, fat 15.3, fiber 0.2, carbs 0.9, protein 70.4

Beef and Artichoke Saute

Preparation time: 10 minutes
Cooking time: 65 minutes
Servings: 4

Ingredients:
- 1 and ½ pounds beef stew meat, cubed
- 6 oz artichoke hearts, chopped
- 1 cup beef broth
- 1 teaspoon Italian seasonings
- 1 garlic clove, peeled
- 1 teaspoon ground nutmeg
- 1 teaspoon coconut oil

Directions:
1. Put all ingredients in the air fryer basket and gently mix.
2. Cook the saute at 350F for 65 minutes.

Nutrition: calories 363, fat 12.7, fiber 2.4, carbs 5.4, protein 54.3

Vinegar Beef Shank

Prep time: 15 minutes
Cooking time: 40 minutes
Servings: 6

Ingredients:
- 3-pound beef shank
- ¼ cup apple cider vinegar
- 1 tablespoon avocado oil
- 1 teaspoon white pepper
- ½ teaspoon salt

Directions:
1. Mix avocado oil with apple cider vinegar, white pepper, and salt.
2. Then sprinkle the beef shank with apple cider vinegar mixture.

3. Put the beef shank in the air fryer basket and cook it at 365F for 40 minutes.

Nutrition: calories 427, fat 14.4, fiber 0.2, carbs 0.5, protein 68.9

Chives Beef

Preparation time: 10 minutes
Cooking time: 35 minutes
Servings: 4

Ingredients:
- 2 oz chives, chopped
- 2-pound beef sirloin, chopped
- 3 tablespoons apple cider vinegar
- 1 tablespoon avocado oil
- ½ teaspoon minced garlic
- 1 teaspoon dried dill

Directions:
1. Sprinkle the beef sirloin in the air fryer.
2. Add apple cider vinegar, minced garlic, dried dill, and chives.
3. Cook the meal at 365F for 35 minutes. Shake the beef every 10 minutes.

Nutrition: calories 434, fat 14.7, fiber 0.5, carbs 1.2, protein 69.4

Thyme Beef

Prep time: 15 minutes
Cooking time: 40 minutes
Servings: 4

Ingredients:
- 1-pound beef sirloin
- 2 tablespoons avocado oil
- 1 teaspoon dried thyme
- 1 teaspoon coconut aminos

Directions:
1. Mix beef sirloin with avocado oil, dried thyme, and coconut aminos.
2. Marinate the beef sirloin for 10 minutes.
3. Then put the meat in the air fryer basket and cook for 40 minutes at 360F.

Nutrition: calories 222, fat 8, fiber 0.4, carbs 0.8, protein 34.5

Marinated Beef

Preparation time: 5 minutes
Cooking time: 75 minutes
Servings: 4

Ingredients:
- ¼ cup apple cider vinegar
- 1 teaspoon dried rosemary
- ½ teaspoon ground coriander
- 1 garlic clove, crushed
- 1 tablespoon olive oil
- 2-pounds beef loin, roughly chopped

Directions:
1. Mix all ingredients in the air fryer and cook the meal at 355F for 75 minutes.

Nutrition: calories 448, fat 22.5, fiber 0.2, carbs 0.6, protein 60.7

Coriander Lamb Steak

Prep time: 10 minutes
Cooking time: 12 minutes
Servings: 2

Ingredients:
- 14 oz lamb steak
- 1 teaspoon ground coriander
- 1 teaspoon garlic powder

- 1 tablespoon olive oil

Directions:
1. Rub the lamb steak with ground coriander, garlic powder, and olive oil.
2. Put the lamb steaks in the air fryer and cook for 6 minutes per side at 385F.

Nutrition: calories 434, fat 21.6, fiber 0.1, carbs 1, protein 56

Lamb Fritters

Preparation time: 15 minutes
Cooking time: 20 minutes
Servings: 8

Ingredients:
- 1 teaspoon onion powder
- 1 teaspoon garlic powder
- ½ teaspoon ground coriander
- 1 teaspoon salt
- 2-pound lamb, minced
- ½ cup cauliflower, shredded
- Cooking spray

Directions:
1. Spray the air fryer basket with cooking spray from inside.
2. Then mix onion powder with garlic powder, ground coriander, salt, lamb, and cauliflower.
3. Make the fritters from the beef mixture and put them in the air fryer.
4. Cook the fritters at 360F for 10 minutes per side.

Nutrition: calories 215, fat 8.3, fiber 0.2, carbs 0.8, protein 32.1

Beef Wraps

Prep time: 10 minutes
Cooking time: 4 minutes

Servings: 5

Ingredients:
- 5 wonton wraps
- 1-pound beef loin, boiled, shredded
- 2 tablespoons marinara sauce
- 1 egg, beaten
- 1 teaspoon olive oil

Directions:
1. Mix shredded beef loin with marinara sauce and egg.
2. Then fill the wonton wraps with beef mixture and wrap them.
3. Brush every wrap with olive oil and cook in the air fryer at 400F for 4 minutes.

Nutrition: calories 201, fat 9.5, fiber 0.2, carbs 2.9, protein 26

Turmeric Lamb Chops

Preparation time: 10 minutes
Cooking time: 16 minutes
Servings: 4

Ingredients:
- 8 lamb chops
- 1 teaspoon ground turmeric
- 1 tablespoon avocado oil
- 1 teaspoon salt
- 3 tablespoons apple cider vinegar

Directions:
1. Sprinkle the lamb chops with ground turmeric, avocado oil, apple cider vinegar, and salt.
2. Put the lamb chops in the air fryer and cook them for 8 minutes per side at 375F.

Nutrition: calories 325, fat 13, fiber 0.3, carbs 0.7, protein 47.8

Lamb with Mint Sauce

Preparation time: 5 minutes
Cooking time: 24 minutes
Servings: 4

Ingredients:
- 8 lamb chops
- 1 teaspoon salt
- 1 tablespoon mint, chopped
- 1 teaspoon garlic powder
- 3 tablespoons lime juice
- ¼ cup of water
- 2 tablespoons avocado oil

Directions:
1. Sprinkle the lamb chops with salt and avocado oil and put in the air fryer.
2. Add mint and garlic powder.
3. Then add water and lime juice.
4. Cook the lamb chops a 375F for 24 minutes.

Nutrition: calories 407, fat 19.6, fiber 1.6, carbs 7.2, protein 48.5

Nutmeg Lamb Chops

Prep time: 15 minutes
Cooking time: 12 minutes
Servings: 4

Ingredients:
- 16 oz lamb chops
- 1 teaspoon ground nutmeg
- 2 tablespoons lemon juice
- 2 tablespoons avocado oil
- ¼ teaspoon salt

Directions:
1. Rub the lamb chops with ground nutmeg, lemon juice, avocado oil, and salt.

2. Put the lamb chops in the air fryer and cook at 385F for 6 minutes per side.

Nutrition: calories 225, fat 9.5, fiber 0.5, carbs 0.8, protein 32

Paprika Lamb Skewers

Preparation time: 10 minutes
Cooking time: 20 minutes
Servings: 4

Ingredients:
- 2-pounds lamb meat, cubed
- 2 tablespoons avocado oil
- 1 teaspoon smoked paprika
- 1 teaspoon chili flakes
- 1 teaspoon keto tomato paste

Directions:
1. Mix lamb meat with avocado oi, smoked paprika, chili flakes, and tomato paste.
2. Then sting the meat into skewers and put in the air fryer.
3. Cook the lamb skewers at 385F for 20 minutes.

Nutrition: calories 319, fat 21, fiber 0.6, carbs 1, protein 32.3

Fennel Rack of Lamb

Prep time: 10 minutes
Cooking time: 30 minutes
Servings: 5

Ingredients:
- 18 oz rack of lamb
- 1 tablespoon fennel seeds
- 2 tablespoons olive oil
- 1 jalapeno pepper, minced
- 2 tablespoons coconut aminos

Directions:
1. In the shallow bowl, mix fennel seeds with olive oil, minced jalapeno pepper, and coconut aminos.
2. Then rub the rack of lamb with jalapeno pepper mixture and put it in the air fryer basket.
3. Cook the meal at 365F for 30 minutes.

Nutrition: calories 230, fat 14.8, fiber 0.5, carbs 2, protein 21

Lamb Chops with Kalamata Spread

Preparation time: 10 minutes
Cooking time: 20 minutes
Servings: 4

Ingredients:
- 4 lamb chops
- 4 kalamata olives, diced
- 1 teaspoon minced garlic
- 1 cup fresh spinach, chopped
- 2 tablespoons olive oil
- 1 tablespoon lemon juice
- ½ teaspoon ground black pepper

Directions:
1. Mix lamb chops with ground black pepper, lemon juice, and olive oil.
2. Put the lamb chops in the air fryer and cook them for 10 minutes per side at 360F.
3. Meanwhile, blend all remaining ingredients until smooth.
4. Top the cooked lamb chops with olives spread.

Nutrition: calories 228, fat 13.8, fiber 0.4, carbs 1, protein 24.2

Pecan Lamb Meatballs

Preparation time: 15 minutes
Cooking time: 35 minutes
Servings: 4

Ingredients:
- 2 pecans, grinded
- 1 oz Provolone, grated
- 2-pound lamb, minced
- 1 teaspoon olive oil
- ½ teaspoon white pepper

Directions:
1. Mix minced lamb with white pepper, grinded pecans, and Provolone.
2. Make the meatballs and put them in the air fryer basket.
3. Sprinkle the meatballs with olive oil and cook at 350F for 35 minutes.

Nutrition: calories 506, fat 24.7, fiber 0.8, carbs 1.3, protein 66.3

Spicy Lamb Sirloin Steak

Prep time: 20 minutes
Cooking time: 35 minutes
Servings: 4

Ingredients:
- 2-pounds lamb sirloin
- 1 teaspoon chili powder
- 1 teaspoon cayenne pepper
- 1 teaspoon minced ginger
- 2 tablespoons avocado oil
- 2 tablespoons coconut cream

Directions:
1. Sprinkle the lamb sirloin with chili powder, cayenne pepper, minced ginger, avocado oil, and coconut cream.
2. Leave the lamb sirloin to marinate for 15 minutes.
3. Then transfer it in the air fryer and cook at 375F for 35 minutes.

Nutrition: calories 494, fat 23.7, fiber 0.9, carbs 1.7, protein 64.7

Lamb and Avocado Bowl

Preparation time: 15 minutes
Cooking time: 35 minutes
Servings: 4

Ingredients:
- 1-pound lamb sirloin, chopped
- ½ teaspoon ground turmeric
- ½ teaspoon ground paprika
- ½ teaspoon chili flakes
- 1 tablespoon olive oil
- 4 tablespoons water
- 1 avocado, pitted, chopped
- 4 tablespoons heavy cream

Directions:
1. Mix lamb sirloin with ground turmeric, ground paprika, chili flakes, olive oil, and water.
2. Put the meat in the air fryer and cook it for 35 minutes at 365F.
3. Then put the meat in the bowl, add avocado and top the meal with heavy cream.

Nutrition: calories 417, fat 29.3, fiber 3.5, carbs 5.1, protein 33.5

Cilantro and Lamb Burgers

Prep time: 15 minutes
Cooking time: 16 minutes
Servings: 2

Ingredients:
- 10 oz lamb fillet, minced
- ¼ cup broccoli, shredded
- 1 tablespoon dried cilantro
- ½ teaspoon onion powder
- 1 teaspoon coconut oil, melted

Directions:
1. Mix minced lamb fillet with broccoli, dried cilantro, and onion powder.
2. Make the burgers.
3. Then sprinkle them with coconut oil and put in the air fryer.
4. Cook the burgers at 360F for 8 minutes per side.

Nutrition: calories 289, fat 12.7, fiber 0.3, carbs 1.3, protein 40.2

Tender Curry Bites

Preparation time: 25 minutes
Cooking time: 30 minutes
Servings: 4

Ingredients:
- 1-pound lamb fillet, cubed
- 1 teaspoon curry paste
- ¼ cup coconut cream
- 1 teaspoon olive oil

Directions:
1. Mix all ingredients in the mixing bowl and leave for 20 minutes to marinate.
2. Then transfer the meat mixture in the air fryer and cook at 365F for 30 minutes.

Nutrition: calories 264, fat 13.8, fiber 0.3, carbs 1.2, protein 32.2

Cilantro Lamb Sausages

Prep time: 25 minutes
Cooking time: 20 minutes
Servings: 4

Ingredients:
- 4 sausage links

- 2-pounds ground lamb
- 1 tablespoon dried cilantro
- 1 teaspoon salt
- 1 tablespoon avocado oil

Directions:
1. Mix ground lamb with dried cilantro and salt.
2. Then fill the sausage links with lamb mixture and brush with avocado oil.
3. Put the sausages in the air fryer and cook for 10 minutes per side at 390F.

Nutrition: calories 477, fat 21.6, fiber 0.2, carbs 0.6, protein 65.7

Caraway Seeds Lamb Loin

Preparation time: 10 minutes
Cooking time: 30 minutes
Servings: 4

Ingredients:
- 2-pound lamb loin
- ½ cup apple cider vinegar
- 1 tablespoon coconut oil, melted
- 1 tablespoon caraway seeds
- ½ teaspoon salt

Directions:
1. Marinate the lamb loin in the mixture of apple cider vinegar, coconut oil, caraway seeds, and salt.
2. Then put the meat in the air fryer and cook it at 375F for 30 minutes.

Nutrition: calories 474, fat 22.8, fiber 0.8, carbs 1.3, protein 60.7

Butter Rack of Lamb

Prep time: 10 minutes
Cooking time: 50 minutes

Servings: 4

Ingredients:
- 16 oz rack of lamb, chopped
- ½ cup butter, softened
- 1 tablespoon dried parsley
- 1 teaspoon salt

Directions:
1. Sprinkle the rack of lamb with dried parsley and salt.
2. Then put the meat in the air fryer and add butter.
3. Cook the meat at 355F for 50 minutes.

Nutrition: calories 472, fat 37.7, fiber 0, carbs 0.1, protein 32.3

Ginger Lamb Cutlets

Preparation time: 10 minutes
Cooking time: 16 minutes
Servings: 4

Ingredients:
- 2-pound lamb cutlets
- 1 teaspoon minced ginger
- 1 tablespoon avocado oil
- ½ teaspoon ground black pepper

Directions:
1. Mix minced ginger with avocado oil and ground black pepper.
2. Mix lamb cutlets with the ginger mixture and cook in the air fryer at 375F for 8 minutes per side.

Nutrition: calories 429, fat 17.1, fiber 0.3, carbs 0.7, protein 63.8

Aromatic London Broil

Prep time: 2 hours
Cooking time: 35 minutes

Servings: 2

Ingredients:
- 12 oz leg of lamb, boneless
- 1 teaspoon dried thyme
- ½ teaspoon dried cilantro
- 1 teaspoon onion powder
- 1 tablespoon coconut aminos
- 1 tablespoon avocado oil

Directions:
1. Mix all ingredients from the list above in the mixing bowl and leave to marinate for 2 hours.
2. Then transfer the meat mixture in the air fryer and cook it at 375F for 35 minutes. Stir the meat from time to time to avoid burning.

Nutrition: calories 339, fat 13.4, fiber 0.6, carbs 3.2, protein 48

Almond and Coconut Meatballs

Preparation time: 15 minutes
Cooking time: 30 minutes
Servings: 4

Ingredients:
- 1 and ½ pounds lamb, ground
- 1 oz almonds, grinded
- 1 tablespoon coconut shred
- 1 teaspoon dried dill
- 1 tablespoon olive oil

Directions:
1. Mix ground lamb with almonds, coconut shred, and dried dill.
2. Make the meatballs and put them in the air fryer.
3. Sprinkle the meatballs with olive oil and cook at 350F for 30 minutes.

Nutrition: calories 398, fat 20.2, fiber 1, carbs 2.7, protein 49.4

Chipotle Rib Eyes

Prep time: 15 minutes
Cooking time: 18 minutes
Servings: 4

Ingredients:
- 1-pound beef rib eye steak, bone-in (4 steaks)
- 1 tablespoon coconut oil
- 1 teaspoon onion powder
- ½ teaspoon lemon zest, grated
- ½ teaspoon ground black pepper
- 1 teaspoon chipotle powder
- 1 teaspoon salt

Directions:
1. In the shallow bowl, mix coconut oil with onion powder, lemon zest, ground black pepper, chipotle powder, and salt.
2. Rub the beef rib-eye steak with the chipotle mixture and put in the air fryer.
3. Cook it at 385F for 9 minutes per side.

Nutrition: calories 303, fat 24.5, fiber 0.1, carbs 0.7, protein 20.2

African Style Lamb

Preparation time: 15 minutes
Cooking time: 50 minutes
Servings: 4

Ingredients:
- 21 oz lamb cutlets
- 1 teaspoon white pepper
- 4 tablespoons avocado oil
- 1 teaspoon dried basil
- 1 tablespoon garlic powder
- 1 tablespoon ground coriander
- 1 tablespoon lemon zest, grated
- 3 tablespoons apple cider vinegar

Directions:
1. Chop the lamb cutlets roughly and put in the air fryer.
2. Add all remaining ingredients and carefully mix the mixture.
3. Cook the meal at 365F for 50 minutes. Stir it after 20 minutes of cooking.

Nutrition: calories 307, fat 12.7, fiber 1.1, carbs 3.1, protein 42.4

Lamb Sticks

Preparation time: 15 minutes
Cooking time: 30 minutes
Servings: 4

Ingredients:
- 1 teaspoon minced garlic
- 1 oz chives, chopped
- 1 teaspoon dried dill
- 2-pound lamb, minced

Directions:
1. Mix lamb mince with dried dill, chives, and minced garlic.
2. Make the sticks from the lamb mixture and put in the air fryer and cook them at 355F for 30 minutes.

Nutrition: calories 426, fat 16.7, fiber 0.2, carbs 0.7, protein 64

Peppermint Lamb

Prep time: 10 minutes
Cooking time: 12 minutes
Servings: 4

Ingredients:
- 1-pound lamb chops
- 1 teaspoon peppermint

- 1 teaspoon avocado oil
- 2 tablespoons lemon juice

Directions:
1. Sprinkle the lamb chops with peppermint, avocado oil, and lemon juice.
2. Put them in the air fryer and cook them for 6 minutes per side at 400F.

Nutrition: calories 215, fat 8.5, fiber 0.1, carbs 0.3, protein 31.9

Tender Clove Lamb

Preparation time: 10 minutes
Cooking time: 30 minutes
Servings: 4

Ingredients:
- 8 lamb cutlets
- 1 teaspoon ground clove
- 1 teaspoon salt
- Cooking spray

Directions:
1. Sprinkle the lamb cutlets with ground clove and salt.
2. Then put them in the air fryer and spray with cooking spray.
3. Cook the lamb cutlets at 360F for 15 minutes per side.

Nutrition: calories 318, fat 12.6, fiber 0.2, carbs 0.3, protein 47.8

Rosemary Leg of Lamb

Prep time: 10 minutes
Cooking time: 30 minutes
Servings: 2

Ingredients:
- 9 oz leg of lamb, boneless
- 1 teaspoon dried rosemary

- 1 teaspoon coconut oil, melted

Directions:
1. Put the leg of lamb in the air fryer.
2. Sprinkle it with dried rosemary and coconut oil.
3. Cook the meal at 365F for 30 minutes.

Nutrition: calories 259, fat 11.7, fiber 0.3, carbs 0.4, protein 35.9

Saffron Lamb Chops

Preparation time: 10 minutes
Cooking time: 20 minutes
Servings: 4

Ingredients:
- 4 lamb chops
- 4 garlic cloves, minced
- 1 teaspoon saffron
- Cooking spray

Directions:
1. Sprinkle the lamb chops with garlic cloves and saffron.
2. Then spray the lamb chops with cooking spray.
3. Put the lamb chops in the air fryer and cook for 10 minutes per side at 360F.

Nutrition: calories 163, fat 6.3, fiber 0.1, carbs 1.1, protein 24.1

Marjoram Lamb Chops

Preparation time: 10 minutes
Cooking time: 25 minutes
Servings: 4

Ingredients:
- 2-pound lamb chops
- 1 teaspoon dried marjoram

- 1 teaspoon salt
- 1 tablespoon coconut cream
- 1 teaspoon coconut oil, melted

Directions:
1. In the shallow bowl, mix dried marjoram, salt, coconut cream, and coconut oil.
2. Carefully rub the lamb chops with marjoram mixture and put it in the air fryer.
3. Cook the lamb chops for 25 minutes at 375F.

Nutrition: calories 441, fat 18.7, fiber 0.1, carbs 0.3, protein 63.8

Garlic Oxtails

Prep time: 5 minutes
Cooking time: 65 minutes
Servings: 5

Ingredients:
- 2-pound beef oxtail, roughly chopped
- 1 teaspoon salt
- 1 cup of water
- 1 teaspoon keto tomato paste
- 1 teaspoon ground black pepper
- 1 teaspoon Erythritol
- 1 teaspoon avocado oil

Directions:
1. Put all ingredients in the air fryer and gently mix.
2. Cook the meal at 360F for 65 minutes.

Nutrition: calories 451, fat 24.1, fiber 0.2, carbs 0.5, protein 56.1

Lamb Sauce

Preparation time: 5 minutes
Cooking time: 30 minutes

Servings: 4

Ingredients:
- 1-pound lamb, minced
- ½ cup heavy cream
- 2 oz Parmesan, grated
- 1 teaspoon coconut oil

Directions:
1. Mix heavy cream with minced lamb and coconut oil and put it in the air fryer.
2. Cook the mixture for 20 minutes at 365F.
3. Then add Parmesan and carefully mix the meal.
4. Cook it at 380F for 10 minutes more.

Nutrition: calories 318, fat 18, fiber 0, carbs 0.9, protein 36.7

Yogurt Lamb Chops

Preparation time: 20 minutes
Cooking time: 375 minutes
Servings: 4

Ingredients:
- 2-pound lamb chops
- 1 cup Plain yogurt
- 1 teaspoon dried thyme
- 1 teaspoon salt
- 1 teaspoon olive oil

Directions:
1. In the mixing bowl, mix Plain yogurt with dried thyme, salt, and olive oil.
2. Put the lamb chops in the yogurt mixture and leave for 10 minutes to marinate.
3. Then put the lamb chops and yogurt mixture in the air fryer and cook for 30 minutes at 375F.

Nutrition: calories 476, fat 18.6, fiber 0.1, carbs 4.5, protein 67.2

Aromatic Lamb Balls

Prep time: 15 minutes
Cooking time: 15 minutes
Servings: 4

Ingredients:
- 1-pound minced lamb
- 1 teaspoon flax meal
- ½ teaspoon chili powder
- 1 egg, beaten
- Cooking spray

Directions:
1. Mix minced lamb with flax meal, chili powder, and egg.
2. Make the balls from the lamb mixture and put it in the air fryer.
3. Then spray the balls with cooking spray and cook them for 15 minutes at 390F.

Nutrition: calories 230, fat 9.7, fiber 0.3, carbs 0.4, protein 33.4

Pork

Garlic Pork Tenderloin

Preparation time: 5 minutes
Cooking time: 25 minutes
Servings: 4

Ingredients:
- 2-pound pork tenderloin
- 1 tablespoon coconut oil, melted
- 1 tablespoon garlic powder
- 1 teaspoon dried dill

Directions:
1. Rub the pork tenderloin with garlic powder and dried dill.
2. Then put the pork tenderloin in the air fryer and sprinkle with coconut oil.
3. Cook the meat at 390F for 25 minutes.

Nutrition: calories 361, fat 11.4, fiber 0.2, carbs 1.7, protein 59.8

Butter Pork Tenderloin

Preparation time: 5 minutes
Cooking time: 30 minutes
Servings: 4

Ingredients:
- 2-pound pork tenderloin, chopped
- ¼ cup butter
- 1 teaspoon chili powder
- ½ teaspoon salt

Directions:
1. Put all ingredients in the air fryer and gently mix.
2. Cook the meat at 390F for 30 minutes.

Nutrition: calories 428, fat 19.6, fiber 0.2, carbs 0.4, protein 59.6

Tender Pork

Prep time: 20 minutes
Cooking time: 40 minutes
Servings: 5

Ingredients:
- 3-pound pork shoulder
- 1 tablespoon cream cheese
- 1 tablespoon avocado oil
- 1 tablespoon lemon juice
- ½ teaspoon salt
- ½ tablespoon cayenne pepper

Directions:
1. In the shallow bowl mix cream cheese with avocado oil, lemon juice, salt, and cayenne pepper.
2. Carefully rub the pork shoulder with cream cheese mixture and leave for 15 minutes to marinate.
3. Then sprinkle the pork shoulder with avocado oil and put it in the air fryer.
4. Cook the pork at 360F for 40 minutes.

Nutrition: calories 808, fat 59.4, fiber 0.3, carbs 0.6, protein 63.6

Vinegar Pork Chops

Preparation time: 10 minutes
Cooking time: 20 minutes
Servings: 4

Ingredients:
- 4 pork chops
- ¼ cup apple cider vinegar
- 1 teaspoon ground black pepper
- 1 teaspoon olive oil

Directions:

1. Mix apple cider vinegar with olive oil and ground black pepper.
2. Then mix pork chops with apple cider vinegar mixture.
3. Put the meat in the air fryer and cook it at 375F for 10 minutes per side.

Nutrition: calories 271, fat 21.1, fiber 0.1, carbs 0.5, protein 18

Pork Stuffing

Prep time: 10 minutes
Cooking time: 35 minutes
Servings: 6

Ingredients:
- 4 oz pork rinds
- 2 pecans, chopped
- 1 teaspoon Italian seasonings
- ½ teaspoon white pepper
- 1 egg, beaten
- 4 tablespoons almond flour
- 3 cups ground pork
- 1 tablespoon avocado oil
- ¼ cup heavy cream

Directions:
1. Put all ingredients in the mixing bowl and stir until homogenous.
2. Then transfer the mixture in the air fryer and cook it at 360F for 35 minutes.
3. Stir the meal every 10 minutes.

Nutrition: calories 667, fat 47.9, fiber 1.2, carbs 2.2, protein 54.9

Dijon Pork Chops

Preparation time: 10 minutes
Cooking time: 20 minutes
Servings: 4

Ingredients:
- 4 pork chops
- 1 tablespoon Dijon mustard
- 1 teaspoon chili powder
- 1 tablespoon avocado oil

Directions:
1. Mix Dijon mustard with chili powder and avocado oil.
2. Then carefully brush the pork chops with the mustard mixture from both sides.
3. Cook the pork chops at 375F for 10 minutes per side.

Nutrition: calories 265, fat 20.6, fiber 0.5, carbs 0.8, protein 18.3

African Style Pork Shoulder

Prep time: 25 minutes
Cooking time: 50 minutes
Servings: 4

Ingredients:
- 2-pound pork shoulder
- 1 teaspoon dried sage
- 1 teaspoon curry powder
- ¼ cup plain yogurt
- 1 tablespoon avocado oil

Directions:
1. Mix curry powder with plain yogurt and avocado oil.
2. Add dried sage and stir the mixture.
3. Then brush the pork shoulder with plain yogurt mixture and leave for 20 minutes to marinate.
4. Then transfer the pork shoulder in the air fryer. Add all remaining yogurt mixture.
5. Cook the meal at 365F for 50 minutes.

Nutrition: calories 680, fat 49.2, fiber 0.4, carbs 1.7, protein 53.8

Scallions Pork Chops

Preparation time: 25 minutes
Cooking time: 20 minutes
Servings: 4

Ingredients:
- 2 tablespoons avocado oil
- 4 pork chops
- 2 oz scallions, minced
- 1 teaspoon onion powder

Directions:
1. In the shallow bowl mix avocado oil with minced scallions and onion powder.
2. Then mix scallions mixture with pork chops and leave for 10-15 minutes to marinate.
3. After this, put the pork chops in the air fryer in one layer and cook at 380F for 10 minutes per side.

Nutrition: calories 272, fat 20.8, fiber 0.7, carbs 1.9, protein 18.4

Taco Pork

Prep time: 10 minutes
Cooking time: 30 minutes
Servings: 6

Ingredients:
- 4-pound pork stew meat
- 1 tablespoon taco seasonings
- 1 tablespoon coconut oil, melted

Directions:
1. Chop the pork stew meat and put it in the skillet.
2. Add coconut oil and roast the meat for 3 minutes per side.

3. Then mix meat with taco seasonings and put in the air fryer.
4. Cook the meat at 365F for 25 minutes.

Nutrition: calories 661, fat 31.5, fiber 0, carbs 0, protein 88.5

Pork Mignons

Preparation time: 10 minutes
Cooking time: 25 minutes
Servings: 4

Ingredients:
- 1-pound pork tenderloin, sliced
- 1 tablespoon olive oil
- 1 teaspoon ground paprika
- ¼ teaspoon ground coriander

Directions:
1. Mix pork tenderloin with olive oil, ground paprika, and ground coriander.
2. Preheat the skillet well and put the sliced pork inside. Cook the meat for 1 minute per side on high heat.
3. Then put pork tenderloin slices in the air fryer and cook them for 10 minutes per side at 365F.

Nutrition: calories 194, fat 7.6, fiber 0.2, carbs 0.3, protein 29.8

Pork Rinds Dip

Prep time: 10 minutes
Cooking time: 30 minutes
Servings: 6

Ingredients:
- 12 oz pork rinds
- ½ cup heavy cream
- 1 cup Mozzarella, shredded
- 1 teaspoon ground coriander
- ¼ teaspoon dried basil

- ½ teaspoon dried sage
- 1 teaspoon avocado oil

Directions:
1. Mix all ingredients in the mixing bowl.
2. Then transfer it in the air fryer and cook at 360F for 30 minutes. Stir the mixture with the help of the spatula every 10 minutes.

Nutrition: calories 373, fat 24.9, fiber 0.1, carbs 0.5, protein 38

Hot Pork

Preparation time: 10 minutes
Cooking time: 16 minutes
Servings: 4

Ingredients:
- 2-pounds pork chops, chopped
- 1 tablespoon keto hot sauce
- 1 teaspoon smoked paprika
- 1 tablespoon coconut oil, melted

Directions:
1. Mix keto hot sauce, smoked paprika, and coconut oil.
2. Then carefully brush the pork chops with hot sauce mixture.
3. Put the pork chops in the hot skillet and roast for 3 minutes per side on medium heat.
4. Then transfer the pork chops in the air fryer and cook them at 375F for 5 minutes per side.

Nutrition: calories 757, fat 59.8, fiber 0.2, carbs 0.3, protein 51

Thyme Pork Chops

Preparation time: 8 minutes
Cooking time: 20 minutes

Servings: 4

Ingredients:
- 4 pork chops
- 1 tablespoon avocado oil
- 1 tablespoon dried thyme

Directions:
1. Sprinkle the pork chops with thyme and avocado oil and put in the air fryer.
2. Cook the pork chops at 380F for 10 minutes per side.

Nutrition: calories 263, fat 20.4, fiber 0.4, carbs 0.6, protein 18.1

Tomato Pork Chops

Preparation time: 10 minutes
Cooking time: 16 minutes
Servings: 4

Ingredients:
- 1 tablespoon keto tomato paste
- 1 tablespoon avocado oil
- 1 teaspoon ground turmeric
- 1 teaspoon ground black pepper
- 4 pork chops

Directions:
1. Mix tomato paste with avocado oil.
2. Then sprinkle the pork chops with ground turmeric and ground black pepper.
3. After this, brush the pork chops with tomato paste and put in the air fryer.
4. Cook the pork chops at 360F for 8 minutes per side.

Nutrition: calories 267, fat 20.4, fiber 0.6, carbs 1.7, protein 18.3

Soft and Sweet Pork Chops

Prep time: 10 minutes
Cooking time: 20 minutes
Servings: 4

Ingredients:
- 2-pound pork chops
- 1 teaspoon Erythritol
- 1 teaspoon cream cheese
- 1 teaspoon cayenne pepper
- 1 tablespoon coconut oil, melted

Directions:
1. Sprinkle the pork chops with Erythritol, cream cheese, cayenne pepper, and coconut oil.
2. Then put the meat in the air fryer in one layer and cook at 365F for 10 minutes per side.

Nutrition: calorie 759, fat 60.1, fiber 0.1, carbs 0.3, protein 51.1

Lime Pork

Preparation time: 10 minutes
Cooking time: 20 minutes
Servings: 4

Ingredients:
- 4 pork chops
- 2 tablespoons lime juice
- ½ teaspoon lime zest, grated
- ¼ teaspoon salt
- ¼ teaspoon ground paprika
- 1 tablespoon avocado oil

Directions:
1. In the mixing bowl, mix lime juice, lime zest, salt, ground paprika, and avocado oil.
2. Rub the pork chops with lime mixture and put it in the air fryer.

3. Cook the lime pork chops at 365F for 20 minutes. Flip them from time to time.

Nutrition: calories 261, fat 20.3, fiber 0.2, carbs 0.3, protein 18

Coriander Pork Tenderloin

Prep time: 10 minutes
Cooking time: 30 minutes
Servings: 4

Ingredients:
- 1-pound pork tenderloin
- 1 tablespoon coriander seeds
- ½ cup of water
- 1 teaspoon salt
- 1 teaspoon peppercorns

Directions:
1. Put pork tenderloin in the air fryer.
2. Add coriander seeds, water, salt, and peppercorns.
3. Cook the meat at 400F for 30 minutes.

Nutrition: calories 164, fat 4, fiber 0.2, carbs 0.4, protein 29.8

Nutmeg Pork

Preparation time: 10 minutes
Cooking time: 22 minutes
Servings: 4

Ingredients:
- 1-pound pork tenderloin, trimmed
- 1 teaspoon ground nutmeg
- ½ teaspoon salt
- ½ teaspoon ground paprika
- 1 teaspoon olive oil

Directions:

1.   Sprinkle the pork tenderloin with ground nutmeg, salt, ground paprika, and olive oil.
2.   Put the meat in the air fryer and cook it for 12 minutes at 400F.
3.   Then flip the meat on another side and cook for 10 minutes more.

Nutrition: calories 176, fat 5.4, fiber 0.2, carbs 0.4, protein 29.8

Cream Pork Chops

Prep time: 10 minutes
Cooking time: 21 minutes
Servings: 4

Ingredients:
• 4 pork chops
• 1 cup heavy cream
• ¼ cup Cheddar cheese, shredded
• 1 teaspoon ground black pepper
• 1 teaspoon salt
• ½ teaspoon avocado oil

Directions:
1.   Preheat the avocado oil in the skillet well.
2.   Sprinkle the pork chops with salt and ground black pepper.
3.   Then put the pork chops in the hot skillet and cook them on high heat for 3 minutes per side.
4.   After this, transfer the pork chops in the air fryer and add heavy cream and Cheddar cheese.
5.   Cook the pork chops at 360F for 15 minutes.

Nutrition: calories 390, fat 33.4, fiber 0.2, carbs 1.3, protein 20.4

Tender Pork Cubes

Preparation time: 15 minutes

Cooking time: 16 minutes
Servings: 4

Ingredients:
•   1-pound pork loin, chopped
•   1 teaspoon ground cumin
•   1 tablespoon coconut cream
•   1 teaspoon olive oil
•   1 teaspoon lemon juice

Directions:
1.   Mix pork loin with ground cumin, coconut cream, and olive oil. Leave the meat for 10 minutes to marinate.
2.   After this, transfer the meat in the air fryer in one layer and cook for 8 minutes per side at 365F.
3.   Sprinkle the cooked pork with lemon juice.

Nutrition: calories 295, fat 18, fiber 0.2, carbs 0.5, protein 31.2

Italian Style Pork Loin

Prep time: 10 minutes
Cooking time: 20 minutes
Servings: 2

Ingredients:
• 12 oz pork loin, sliced
• 1 tablespoon Italian seasonings
• 1 tablespoon avocado oil

Directions:
1.   Sprinkle the pork loin with Italian seasonings and avocado oil.
2.   Then put the pork loin slices in the air fryer in one layer and cook at 400F for 20 minutes.

Nutrition: calories 442, fat 26.7, fiber 0.3, carbs 1.2, protein 46.6

Cheesy Pork Rolls

Preparation time: 15 minutes
Cooking time: 20 minutes
Servings: 4

Ingredients:
- 4 pork chops
- 4 slices Cheddar cheese
- 1 teaspoon ground black pepper
- 1 teaspoon olive oil
- 1 teaspoon dried basil

Directions:
1. Sprinkle the pork chops with ground black pepper and dried basil.
2. Then top the meat with Cheddar cheese slices and roll into rolls. Secure the pork rolls with toothpicks if needed.
3. Then preheat the olive oil in the skillet well.
4. Add the pork rolls and cook on high heat for 2 minutes per side.
5. Then transfer the pork rolls in the air fryer and cook the meal at 400F for 8 minutes per side.

Nutrition: calories 380, fat 30.4, fiber 0.1, carbs 0.7, protein 25

Marinara Pork Tenderloin

Prep time: 10 minutes
Cooking time: 30 minutes
Servings: 3

Ingredients:
- 12 oz pork tenderloin
- ½ cup marinara sauce
- 1 teaspoon olive oil

Directions:
1. Mix pork tenderloin with olive oil and put it in the air fryer.
2. Top the meat with marinara sauce and cook for 30 minutes at 375F.

Nutrition: calories 212, fat 6.7, fiber 1.1, carbs 5.7, protein 30.4

Oregano Pork Chops

Preparation time: 10 minutes
Cooking time: 18 minutes
Servings: 4

Ingredients:
- 4 pork chops
- 1 tablespoon dried oregano
- ½ teaspoon minced garlic
- 2 tablespoons olive oil

Directions:
1. Heat the pan well and put the pork chops inside.
2. Roast them for 2 minutes per side and transfer in the air fryer.
3. Sprinkle the meat with dried oregano and minced garlic.
4. Cook the pork chops at 365F for 7 minutes per side.

Nutrition: calories 320, fat 20.7, fiber 0.5, carbs 0.9, protein 18.1

Wrapped Pork Tenderloin

Prep time: 15 minutes
Cooking time: 16 minutes
Servings: 2

Ingredients:
- 12 oz pork tenderloin
- 2 oz bacon, sliced
- 1 teaspoon ground paprika
- ½ teaspoon chili powder

Directions:
1. Rub the pork tenderloin with ground paprika and chili powder.
2. Then wrap the meat in the bacon and put in the air fryer.

3. Cook the meat at 375F for 8 minutes per side.

Nutrition: calories 402, fat 18.1, fiber 0.6, carbs 1.4, protein 55.3

Cinnamon Pork Chops

Preparation time: 10 minutes
Cooking time: 20 minutes
Servings: 4

Ingredients:
- 4 pork chops
- 1 teaspoon ground cinnamon
- 1 teaspoon olive oil
- ½ teaspoon salt

Directions:
1. Rub the pork chops with ground cinnamon, olive oil, and salt.
2. Put the pork chops in the air fryer and cook them for 8-9 minutes per side at 375F.

Nutrition: calories 267, fat 21.1, fiber 0.3, carbs 0.5, protein 18

Coated Pork Chops

Prep time: 15 minutes
Cooking time: 16 minutes
Servings: 4

Ingredients:
- 4 pork chops
- 1 egg, beaten
- 3 tablespoons coconut shred
- 1 teaspoon salt
- Cooking spray

Directions:
1. Sprinkle the pork chops with salt and dip in the egg.
2. Then coat the pork chops in the coconut shred and put in the air fryer.

3. Spray the pork chops with cooking spray and cook them at 375F for 8 minutes.

Nutrition: calories 309, fat 24.7, fiber 0.8, carbs 1.6, protein 19.4

Pork Skewers

Preparation time: 20 minutes
Cooking time: 20 minutes
Servings: 4

Ingredients:
- 1-pound pork loin, chopped
- 1 tablespoon avocado oil
- 3 tablespoons apple cider vinegar
- 1 teaspoon coconut cream
- 1 teaspoon ground black pepper
- ½ teaspoon salt

Directions:
1. In the shallow bowl, mix avocado oil with apple cider vinegar, coconut cream, ground black pepper, and salt.
2. Then mix pork loin with avocado oil mixture and leave for 10 minutes to marinate.
3. Sting the meat into skewers and put in the air fryer.
4. Cook them at 400F for 20 minutes. Flip the skewers from time to time.

Nutrition: calories 286, fat 16.6, fiber 0.3, carbs 0.7, protein 31.1

Thyme Pork Sausages

Prep time: 10 minutes
Cooking time: 25 minutes
Servings: 4

Ingredients:
- 2-pounds pork sausages
- 1 tablespoon dried thyme

- 1 teaspoon olive oil
- 1 teaspoon salt

Directions:
1. Sprinkle the pork sausages with dried thyme, olive oil, and salt.
2. Put the pork sausages in the air fryer.
3. Cook the meal at 375F for 25 minutes. Flip the pork sausages after 15 minutes of cooking.

Nutrition: calories 781, fat 65.5, fiber 0.3, carbs 0.4, protein 44.1

Chili Pork

Preparation time: 10 minutes
Cooking time: 18 minutes
Servings: 2

Ingredients:
- 1-pound pork stew meat, cut into strips
- 1 chili pepper, chopped
- 1 teaspoon salt
- 1 teaspoon olive oil
- ½ teaspoon white pepper

Directions:
1. Brush the air fryer basket with olive oil from inside.
2. Then put the pork strips in the air fryer in one layer.
3. Sprinkle the pork with salt, chili pepper, and white pepper.
4. Cook the meat at 385F for 18 minutes.

Nutrition: calories 503, fat 24.3, fiber 0.2, carbs 0.5, protein 66.5

Cajun Pork Shoulder

Prep time: 10 minutes

Cooking time: 30 minutes
Servings: 4

Ingredients:
- 2-pound pork shoulder, boneless
- 1 tablespoon Cajun seasonings
- 1 tablespoon coconut oil, melted

Directions:
1. Sprinkle the pork shoulder with Cajun seasonings and rub with coconut oil.
2. Then put the meat in the air fryer and cook it for 15 minutes per side at 375F.

Nutrition: calories 692, fat 51.9, fiber 0, carbs 0, protein 52.8

Cumin Spare Ribs

Preparation time: 10 minutes
Cooking time: 24 minutes
Servings: 4

Ingredients:
- 2-pound pork spare ribs, roughly chopped
- 1 tablespoon ground cumin
- 1 teaspoon salt
- 1 tablespoon avocado oil

Directions:
1. Mix avocado oil with salt and ground cumin.
2. After this, sprinkle the pork spare ribs with cumin mixture and transfer in the air fryer.
3. Cook the meal at 385F for 12 minutes per side.

Nutrition: calories 436, fat 29.1, fiber 0.3, carbs 0.9, protein 40.8

Provolone Pork Cutlets

Prep time: 10 minutes
Cooking time: 25 minutes
Servings: 4

Ingredients:
- 12 oz pork cutlets
- 2 oz Provolone, grated
- 1 tablespoon coconut flour
- ½ teaspoon cayenne pepper
- 1 tablespoon coconut oil, melted

Directions:
1. Mix pork cutlets with coconut oil and put in the air fryer.
2. Then sprinkle the meat with cayenne pepper and cook them for 5 minutes per side at 400F.
3. After this, mix Provolone cheese with coconut flour.
4. Top the pork cutlets with cheese mixture and cook for 15 minutes at 350F.

Nutrition: calories 198, fat 13.7, fiber 1.8, carbs 11, protein 7.8

Sweet Pork Ribs

Preparation time: 10 minutes
Cooking time: 20 minutes
Servings: 4

Ingredients:
- 2-pound pork ribs, roughly chopped
- 1 tablespoon Truvia
- ¼ cup apple cider vinegar
- 1 teaspoon white pepper
- 1 tablespoon olive oil
- ½ teaspoon sage

Directions:

1. In the shallow bowl, mix Truvia, apple cider vinegar, white pepper, olive oil, and sage.
2. Then put the pork ribs in the air fryer and sprinkle with Truvia mixture. Gently shake the pork ribs and cook them at 375F for 10 minutes per side.

Nutrition: calories 654, fat 43.7, fiber 0.2, carbs 0.5, protein 60.2

Five Spices Pork

Prep time: 10 minutes
Cooking time: 18 minutes
Servings: 6

Ingredients:
- 2-pound pork shoulder, boneless
- 1 teaspoon salt
- 1 tablespoon five spices powder
- 1 tablespoon avocado oil
- 1 teaspoon chili powder

Directions:
1. Mix pork shoulder with salt, five spices powder, and chili powder.
2. Then sprinkle the meat with avocado oil and put it in the air fryer.
3. Cook the meat at 390F for 18 minutes.

Nutrition: calories 446, fat 32.7, fiber 0.3, carbs 0.4, protein 35.3

Ginger Pork

Preparation time: 10 minutes
Cooking time: 14 minutes
Servings: 4

Ingredients:
- 1 pound pork tenderloin, cut into strips
- 1 tablespoon minced ginger

- 1 tablespoon olive oil

Directions:
1. Mix the minced ginger with olive oil.
2. Sprinkle the pork strips with the ginger mixture and put it in the air fryer.
3. Cook the meat at 380F for 7 minutes per side.

Nutrition: calories 197, fat 7.6, fiber 0.2, carbs 1, protein 29.8

Garlic Pork Ribs

Prep time: 10 minutes
Cooking time: 30 minutes
Servings: 4

Ingredients:
- 1-pound pork baby back ribs
- 1 teaspoon garlic powder
- 1 teaspoon ground coriander
- 1 tablespoon olive oil

Directions:
1. Sprinkle the pork ribs with garlic powder, ground coriander, and olive oil.
2. Put the pork ribs in the air fryer and cook them for 30 minutes at 355F.

Nutrition: calories 446, fat 37.3, fiber 0.1, carbs 0.5, protein 25.8

Classic Schnitzel

Prep time: 15 minutes
Cooking time: 10 minutes
Servings: 2

Ingredients:
- 10 oz pork cutlets
- 1 teaspoon olive oil
- 1 egg, beaten

- 1 tablespoon coconut cream
- ½ cup almond flour
- ½ teaspoon white pepper
- ½ teaspoon salt

Directions:
1. Beat the pork cutlets gently with the help of the kitchen hammer.
2. Then mix salt with almond flour, and white pepper.
3. Dip the pork cutlets in the egg and then coat in the almond flour mixture.
4. Then put the schnitzels in the air fryer and sprinkle with coconut cream and olive oil.
5. Cook the meat at 400F for 5 minutes per side.

Nutrition: calories 423, fat 30.1, fiber 4.9, carbs 10.7, protein 15.5

Chili Pork Ribs

Prep time: 10 minutes
Cooking time: 16 minutes
Servings: 4

Ingredients:
- 1-pound pork ribs, chopped
- 1 teaspoon salt
- 1 teaspoon chili flakes
- 1 teaspoon olive oil

Directions:
1. Mix pork ribs with all remaining ingredients and put in the air fryer basket.
2. Cook the chili pork ribs at 375F for 8 minutes per side.

Nutrition: calories 320, fat 21.3, fiber 0, carbs 0, protein 30.1

Tender Pork Belly

Prep time: 10 minutes

Cooking time: 40 minutes
Servings: 6

Ingredients:
- 1-pound pork belly
- 1 teaspoon white pepper
- 1 teaspoon salt
- 1 teaspoon coconut oil, melted
- ½ teaspoon ground turmeric

Directions:
1. Rub the pork belly with white pepper, salt, coconut oil, and ground nutmeg.
2. Put the pork belly in the air fryer and cook at 365F for 40 minutes.

Nutrition: calories 357, fat 21.1, fiber 0.1, carbs 0.4, protein 34.9

Adobo Pork Chops

Prep time: 10 minutes
Cooking time: 20 minutes
Servings: 5

Ingredients:
- 5 pork chops
- 1 tablespoon adobo seasonings
- 1 tablespoon coconut cream
- 1 teaspoon olive oil

Directions:
1. Rub the pork chops with adobo seasonings, coconut cream, and olive oil.
2. Put the pork chops in the air fryer and cook for 10 minutes per side at 350F.

Nutrition: calories 271, fat 21.5, fiber 0.1, carbs 0.2, protein 18.1

Splenda Pork Ribs

Prep time: 10 minutes
Cooking time: 18 minutes
Servings: 4

Ingredients:
- 12 oz pork ribs, boneless
- 1 tablespoon ranch dressing
- 1 teaspoon Splenda
- 1 tablespoon coconut oil, softened
- ½ teaspoon garlic powder

Directions:
1. Mix ranch seasonings with Splenda, coconut oil, and garlic powder.
2. Then put the pork ribs in the air fryer and sprinkle with Splenda mixture.
3. Cook the meat at 360F for 9 minutes per side.

Nutrition: calories 269, fat 18.5, fiber 0, carbs 1.5, protein 22.6

Pepper Pork Steak

Prep time: 10 minutes
Cooking time: 16 minutes
Servings: 4

Ingredients:
- 16 oz pork steak
- 1 tablespoon ground black pepper
- 1 tablespoon olive oil

Directions:
1. Sprinkle the pork steak with ground black pepper and olive oil and put in the air fryer.
2. Cook it for 8 minutes per side at 400F.

Nutrition: calories 328, fat 22.4, fiber 0.4, carbs 1, protein 29.2

Prosciutto Pork Loin

Prep time: 10 minutes
Cooking time: 15 minutes
Servings: 4

Ingredients:
- 1-pound pork loin
- 3 oz prosciutto, chopped
- 1 tablespoon avocado oil
- 1 teaspoon ground cumin
- ½ teaspoon salt

Directions:
1. Sprinkle the pork loin with avocado oil, ground cumin, and salt.
2. Then wrap the meat with prosciutto and put in the air fryer.
3. Cook the meat at 380F for 15 minutes.

Nutrition: calorie 312, fat 17.5, fiber 0.2, carbs 0.8, protein 35.6

Mustard Ribs

Prep time: 30 minutes
Cooking time: 40 minutes
Servings: 4

Ingredients:
- 2-pound pork ribs, roughly chopped
- 2 tablespoons mustard
- 1 tablespoon olive oil
- 1 tablespoon lemon juice

Directions:
1. Brush the pork ribs with mustard, olive oil, and lemon juice.
2. Put the pork ribs in the air fryer and cook them at 355F for 40 minutes.

Nutrition: calories 676, fat 45.3, fiber 0.8, carbs 2, protein 61.5

Lemon Pork Belly

Prep time: 15 minutes
Cooking time: 55 minutes
Servings: 6

Ingredients:
- 1-pound pork belly
- 1 teaspoon lemon zest, grated
- 2 tablespoons lemon juice
- ½ teaspoon salt
- ½ teaspoon chili powder

Directions:
1. Rub the pork belly with lemon zest, lemon juice, salt, and chili powder.
2. Put it in the air fryer and cook at 350F for 55 minutes.

Nutrition: calories 351, fat 20.4, fiber 0.1, carbs 0.3, protein 35

Keto Onion Pork Cubes

Preparation time: 5 minutes
Cooking time: 18 minutes
Servings: 4

Ingredients:
- 1 pound pork stew meat, cubed
- 1 teaspoon onion powder
- 1 oz scallions, chopped
- 1 tablespoon olive oil
- ½ teaspoon white pepper
- ½ teaspoon salt

Directions:
1. Put all ingredients in the air fryer and gently mix.
2. Cook the pork cubes at 360F for 9 minutes per side,

Nutrition: calories 275, fat 14.5, fiber 0.3, carbs 1.2, protein 33.4

Italian Meatballs

Prep time: 10 minutes
Cooking time: 20 minutes
Servings: 4

Ingredients:
- 2-pound ground pork
- 1 teaspoon dried oregano
- 1 teaspoon dried thyme
- 1 tablespoon olive oil
- ½ teaspoon salt

Directions:
1. In the mixing bowl, mix ground pork with dried oregano, thyme, and salt.
2. Make the meatballs and put them in the air fryer.
3. Sprinkle the meatballs with olive oil and cook at 360F for 20 minutes.

Nutrition: calories 356, fat 11.5, fiber 0.3, carbs 0.4, protein 59.4

Tomatillo and Pork Bowl

Preparation time: 10 minutes
Cooking time: 15 minutes
Servings: 4

Ingredients:
- 12 oz ground pork
- 1 teaspoon Italian seasonings
- 1 teaspoon butter, softened
- 1 teaspoon salt
- 2 tomatillos, chopped

Directions:
1. Put all ingredients except tomatillos in the air fryer.
2. Cook it at 360F for 10 minutes.
3. Then ix the ground pork and add tomatillos.

4. Cook the meal for 5 minutes more at 400F.

Nutrition: calories 139, fat4.5, fiber 0.3, carbs 1.1, protein 22.4

Ground Pork Salad

Prep time: 10 minutes
Cooking time: 15 minutes
Servings: 3

Ingredients:
- 1 cup lettuce, chopped
- 2 cups ground pork
- 1 teaspoon chili flakes
- 1 teaspoon avocado oil
- 2 oz Feta cheese, crumbled
- ½ teaspoon salt

Directions:
1. Mix ground pork with chili flakes and salt.
2. Put it in the air fryer and cook at 360F for 15 minutes. Stir it from time to time.
3. Then transfer the cooked ground pork in the salad bowl.
4. Add all remaining ingredients and gently mix.

Nutrition: calories 674, fat 47.6, fiber 0.2, carbs 1.4, protein 56.4

Zucchini and Pork Stew

Preparation time: 5 minutes
Cooking time: 40 minutes
Servings: 4

Ingredients:
- 2 pounds pork stew meat, cubed
- 1 zucchini, chopped
- 1 teaspoon keto tomato paste
- 1 teaspoon peppercorns

- 1 cup of water
- 1 teaspoon salt

Directions:
1. Put all ingredients in the air fryer and gently mix.
2. Cook the stew at 350F for 40 minutes.

Nutrition: calories 491, fat 22, fiber 0.7, carbs 2.2, protein 67.1

Green Beans and Pork Bowl

Preparation time: 5 minutes
Cooking time: 30 minutes
Servings: 4

Ingredients:
- 1-pound pork tenderloin, chopped
- 1 cup green beans, chopped
- 1 teaspoon ground black pepper
- 1 tablespoon coconut oil
- ¼ cup heavy cream
- 1 teaspoon onion powder

Directions:
1. Put all ingredients except the green beans in the air fryer.
2. Cook the mixture at 370F for 20 minutes.
3. Then add green beans and cook the meat for 10 minutes more.

Nutrition: calories 229, fat 10.2, fiber 1.1, carbs 3, protein 30.5

Cauliflower Salad with Bacon

Prep time: 10 minutes
Cooking time: 6 minutes
Servings: 2

Ingredients:
- 1 cup cauliflower, chopped
- 1 teaspoon avocado oil
- 1 pecan, chopped
- 4 bacon slices
- ½ teaspoon salt
- ½ teaspoon lime zest, grated
- ½ teaspoon sesame oil

Directions:
1. Put the cauliflower, avocado oil, and lemon zest in the air fryer.
2. Add bacon slices and cook the ingredients for 6 minutes at 400F.
3. Then transfer the cooked ingredients in the salad bowl.
4. Add pecan, salt, and sesame oil.
5. Carefully mix the salad.

Nutrition: calories 280, fat 22.4, fiber 2.2, carbs 4.4, protein 15.9

Cajun Pork Casserole

Prep time: 10 minutes
Cooking time: 30 minutes
Servings: 6

Ingredients:
- 1 tablespoon cajun seasonings
- 2 cups ground pork
- 1 cup Mozzarella, shredded
- ¼ cup marinara sauce
- 1 teaspoon olive oil
- ½ cup bell pepper, chopped

Directions:
1. Brush the air fryer basket with olive oil.
2. Then mix ground pork with Cajun seasonings and put in the air fryer.
3. Top the ground pork with marinara sauce, bell pepper, and Mozzarella.
4. Cook the casserole at 390F for 30 minutes.

Nutrition: calories 191, fat 5.8, fiber 0.4, carbs 2.4, protein 30.7

Jalapeno Pork Stew

Preparation time: 5 minutes
Cooking time: 25 minutes
Servings: 4

Ingredients:
- 1 ½ pound pork stew meat, cubed
- 2 jalapenos, chopped
- 1 cup of water
- 1 teaspoon peppercorns
- 1 teaspoon salt

Directions:
1. Put all ingredients in the air fryer and gently mix.
2. Cook the stew at 360F for 25 minutes.

Nutrition: calories 364, fat 16.5, fiber 0.3, carbs 0.8, protein 49.9

Bacon Eggplant

Prep time: 10 minutes
Cooking time: 10 minutes
Servings: 2

Ingredients:
- 1 eggplant, trimmed
- 4 bacon slices
- ½ teaspoon salt
- 1 tablespoon olive oil

Directions:
1. Cut the eggplant into halves and rub it with salt and olive oil.
2. Then top the eggplant with bacon and put in the air fryer.
3. Cook the meal at 400F for 10 minutes.

Nutrition: calories 323, fat 23.3, fiber 8.1, carbs 14, protein 16.3

Spinach Rolls

Preparation time: 10 minutes
Cooking time: 30 minutes
Servings: 4

Ingredients:
- 2 cups ground pork
- 1 teaspoon taco seasonings
- 1 teaspoon olive oil
- 2 cups fresh spinach

Directions:
1. Mix taco seasonings with ground pork.
2. After this, fill every spinach leaf with ground pork mixture, roll, and sprinkle with olive oil.
3. Put the rolls in the air fryer and cook them for 30 minutes at 350F.

Nutrition: calories 483, fat 33.7, fiber 0.3, carbs 1.5, protein 40.6

Pork and Cauliflower Rice

Prep time: 10 minutes
Cooking time: 20 minutes
Servings: 4

Ingredients:
- 1 cup cauliflower, shredded
- 1 cup ground pork
- 1 teaspoon chili flakes
- 1 tablespoon olive oil
- ½ cup heavy cream
- 1 oz Parmesan, grated

Directions:
1. In the mixing bowl, mix cauliflower with ground pork, chili flakes, olive oil, and heavy cream.

2. Put the mixture in the air fryer and cook at 360F for 20 minutes.
3. Then carefully mix the meal and top with Parmesan.

Nutrition: calories 343, fat 26.9, fiber 0.6, carbs 2, protein 23.2

Stuffed Okra

Preparation time: 15 minutes
Cooking time: 20 minutes
Servings: 4

Ingredients:
- 10 oz okra, trimmed, seeded
- 1 cup ground pork
- ½ cup Cheddar cheese, shredded
- 1 teaspoon white pepper
- ½ cup of water

Directions:
1. Mix ground pork with Cheddar cheese and white pepper.
2. Then fill okra with ground pork mixture and transfer in the air fryer.
3. Add water and cook the meal at 370F for 20 minutes.

Nutrition: calories 144, fat 8.8, fiber 2.4, carbs 5.8, protein 10

Tomato Pork Mince

Prep time: 10 minutes
Cooking time: 20 minutes
Servings: 3

Ingredients:
- 2 cups ground pork
- 1 tablespoon keto tomato paste
- 1 teaspoon dried rosemary
- ½ teaspoon salt
- ½ cup coconut cream
- 1 teaspoon butter

Directions:
1. Put all ingredients in the air fryer basket and gently mix.
2. Cook the pork mince at 375F for 20 minutes. Stir the meal after 10 minutes of cooking.

Nutrition: calories 262, fat 21.6, fiber 1.3, carbs 3.5, protein 14.5

Pork and Cabbage Casserole

Preparation time: 10 minutes
Cooking time: 30 minutes
Servings: 4

Ingredients:
- 1 cup white cabbage, shredded
- 2 cups ground pork
- 1 teaspoon chili flakes
- 1 oz scallions, chopped
- ½ cup of water
- 2 oz Parmesan, grated

Directions:
1. Pour water in the air fryer.
2. Then mix ground pork with chili flakes and scallions.
3. Put the mixture in the air fryer and top it with white cabbage and parmesan.
4. Cook the casserole at 365F for 30 minutes.

Nutrition: calories 167, fat 11.1, fiber 0.6, carbs 2.1, protein 14.9

Stuffed Bell Peppers

Prep time: 10 minutes
Cooking time: 20 minutes
Servings: 5

Ingredients:

- 5 bell peppers, trimmed, seeded
- 2 cups ground pork
- 1 teaspoon ground black pepper
- 2 oz scallions, chopped
- 1 teaspoon cream cheese
- ½ cup of water
- 1 teaspoon olive oil

Directions:
1. Mix ground pork with ground black pepper, scallions, and cream cheese.
2. Then fill the bell peppers with ground pork mixture and put in the air fryer.
3. Add water and olive oil and cook the meal at 400F for 20 minutes.

Nutrition: calories 145, fat 7.9, fiber 2, carbs 10.1, protein 9.5

Pork and Brussel Sprouts Hash

Preparation time: 10 minutes
Cooking time: 25 minutes
Servings: 4

Ingredients:
- 12 oz Brussel Sprouts, shredded
- 2 cups ground pork
- 1 teaspoon salt
- 1 teaspoon cayenne pepper
- ½ cup coconut cream
- 1 teaspoon dried oregano
- 1 teaspoon dried cilantro

Directions:
1. In the mixing bowl, mix ground pork with Brussel sprouts, salt, cayenne pepper, coconut cream, dried oregano, and dried cilantro.
2. Cook the hash at 400F for 10 minutes.
3. Then stir it well and cook it for 15 minutes more.

Nutrition: calories 223, fat 15.6, fiber 4.1, carbs 9.9, protein 13.7

Saffron Pork

Preparation time: 10 minutes
Cooking time: 25 minutes
Servings: 4

Ingredients:
- 2-pound pork tenderloin, chopped
- 1 teaspoon saffron
- 1 tablespoon lemon juice
- ½ teaspoon salt
- 1 teaspoon ground coriander

Directions:
1. Mix saffron with lemon juice, salt, and ground coriander.
2. Then sprinkle the pork tenderloin with the lemon juice mixture and put it in the air fryer.
3. Cook the meal at 360F for 25 minutes. Shake the meat every 5 minutes.

Nutrition: calories 326, fat 8, fiber 0, carbs 0.2, protein 59.4

Pork Meatloaf

Prep time: 10 minutes
Cooking time: 16 minutes
Servings: 2

Ingredients:
- 2 cups ground pork
- 1 pecan, grinded
- 1 egg, beaten
- 3 oz Parmesan, grated
- ½ teaspoon chili powder
- 1 teaspoon olive oil

Directions:

1. Brush the air fryer basket with olive oil.
2. Then mix pecan with ground pork, Parmesan, egg, and chili powder.
3. Put the ground pork mixture in the air fryer and flatten it well in the shape of the meatloaf.
4. Cook the meatloaf at 400F for 16 minutes.

Nutrition: calories 469, fat 34.7, fiber 1, carbs 3.1, protein 37.3

Vegetable

Mozzarella Asparagus

Preparation time: 5 minutes
Cooking time: 10 minutes
Servings: 4

Ingredients:
- 1-pound asparagus, roughly chopped
- 1 teaspoon olive oil
- ½ teaspoon ground black pepper
- 2 oz Parmesan, grated

Directions:
1. Mix asparagus with olive oil and ground black pepper and put in the air fryer basket.
2. Cook it at 400F for 8 minutes.
3. Then top the asparagus with Parmesan and cook the meal for 2 minutes more.

Nutrition: calories 79, fat 4.4, fiber 2.5, carbs 5.1, protein 7.1

Roasted Radish Halves

Prep time: 10 minutes
Cooking time: 5 minutes
Servings: 3

Ingredients:
- 2 cups radish, halved
- 1 teaspoon dried rosemary
- 1 tablespoon coconut oil, melted

Directions:
1. Mix radish with dried rosemary and coconut oil.
2. Put the radish in the air fryer basket and cook at 380F for 5 minutes.

Nutrition: calories 53, fat 4.7, fiber 1.4, carbs 2.9, protein 0.6

Paprika Asparagus

Preparation time: 5 minutes
Cooking time: 10 minutes
Servings: 4

Ingredients:
- 1-pound asparagus, trimmed
- 4 Cheddar cheese slices
- 1 teaspoon ground paprika
- 1 teaspoon salt
- 1 tablespoon avocado oil

Directions:
1. Mix asparagus with ground paprika, salt, and avocado oil.
2. Then cut the cheese slices into the strips.
3. Wrap the asparagus in the cheese and put it in the air fryer.
4. Cook the meal at 400F for 10 minutes.

Nutrition: calories 142, fat 9.9, fiber 2.7, carbs 5.3, protein 9.6

Parmesan Latkes

Prep time: 15 minutes
Cooking time: 10 minutes
Servings: 5

Ingredients:
- 2 zucchinis, trimmed, grated
- 3 oz Parmesan, grated
- ½ cup coconut flour
- 1 teaspoon ground turmeric
- 1 teaspoon olive oil

Directions:

1. In the mixing bowl, mix grated zucchini with Parmesan, coconut flour, and ground turmeric.
2. Brush the air fryer basket with olive oil from inside and put the latkes.
3. Cook them for 5 minutes per side at 385F.

Nutrition: calories 125, fat 6, fiber 5.8, carbs 11.5, protein 8.1

Tender Asparagus in Cream Sauce

Preparation time: 5 minutes
Cooking time: 10 minutes
Servings: 4

Ingredients:
- 1-pound asparagus, chopped
- ½ cup heavy cream
- ½ cup Mozzarella, shredded
- 1 teaspoon olive oil
- 1 teaspoon ground black pepper

Directions:
1. Sprinkle the asparagus with olive oil and ground black pepper and put in the air fryer.
2. Cook the asparagus at 400F for 10 minutes.
3. Meanwhile, mix heavy cream with Mozzarella and bring the liquid to boil.
4. Put the asparagus on the serving plate and top it with cream sauce.

Nutrition: calories 96, fat 7.5, fiber 2.5, carbs 5.3, protein 3.9

Swiss Chard Patties

Prep time: 15 minutes
Cooking time: 6 minutes
Servings: 2

Ingredients:
- 1 cup swiss chard, chopped
- 1 zucchini, grated
- 2 tablespoons almond flour
- 1 egg, beaten
- 1 teaspoon olive oil
- 1 teaspoon salt

Directions:
1. In the mixing bowl, mix swiss chard with zucchini, almond flour, egg, and salt.
2. Make the patties from the mixture.
3. Then brush the air fryer basket with olive oil from inside and put the patties there.
4. Cook the meal at 400F for 3 minutes per side.

Nutrition: calories 113, fat 8.1, fiber 2.1, carbs 5.6, protein 5.8

Bacon Asparagus

Preparation time: 5 minutes
Cooking time: 10 minutes
Servings: 4

Ingredients:
- 1-pound asparagus, trimmed
- 2 oz bacon, sliced
- 1 teaspoon avocado oil
- ½ teaspoon salt

Directions:
1. Wrap the asparagus in the bacon slices and sprinkle with avocado oil and salt.
2. Put the vegetables in the air fryer and cook at 400F for 10 minutes.

Nutrition: calories 101, fat 6.2, fiber 2.4, carbs 4.7, protein 7.8

Snap Peas Mash

Prep time: 10 minutes
Cooking time: 6 minutes
Servings: 4

Ingredients:
- 1 cup snap peas, frozen
- 2 oz Provolone, shredded
- 1 teaspoon coconut oil
- ½ teaspoon chili powder
- ¼ cup chicken stock

Directions:
1. Mix snap peas with coconut oil and chicken stock and put in the air fryer.
2. Cook them for 6 minutes at 400F.
3. After this, transfer the snap peas in the blender, add all remaining ingredients and blend until smooth.

Nutrition: calories 90, fat 5.2, fiber 2, carbs 5.8, protein 5.7

Prosciutto Asparagus Mix

Preparation time: 5 minutes
Cooking time: 10 minutes
Servings: 4

Ingredients:
- 2-pounds asparagus, trimmed
- 2 tablespoons avocado oil
- 1 cup Mozzarella cheese, shredded
- 2 oz prosciutto, chopped

Directions:
1. Mix asparagus with avocado oil and put it in the air fryer.
2. Then top the vegetables with mozzarella and prosciutto.
3. Cook the meal at 400F for 10 minutes.

Nutrition: calories 95, fat 3.2, fiber 5.1, carbs 9., protein 10.1

Garlic Fennel Bulb

Prep time: 10 minutes
Cooking time: 15 minutes
Servings: 2

Ingredients:
- 10 oz fennel bulb
- 1 teaspoon avocado oil
- 1 teaspoon garlic powder

Directions:
1. Chop the fennel bulb roughly and sprinkle with avocado oil and garlic powder.
2. Put the fennel bulb in the air fryer and cook at 375F for 15 minutes.

Nutrition: calories 52, fat 0.6, fiber 4.6, carbs 11.5, protein 2

Dijon Mustard Asparagus

Preparation time: 5 minutes
Cooking time: 12 minutes
Servings: 4

Ingredients:
- 1-pound asparagus, trimmed
- 2 tablespoons Dijon mustard
- 1 tablespoon olive oil
- 1 teaspoon lemon juice

Directions:
1. In the shallow bowl, mix Dijon mustard with olive oil, and lemon juice.
2. Then mix asparagus with mustard mixture and put in the air fryer basket.
3. Cook the meal at 400F for 10 minutes.
4. Then shake the asparagus well and cook it for 2 minutes more.

Nutrition: calories 58, fat 4, fiber 2.7, carbs 4.9, protein 2.8

Cheesy Okra

Prep time: 10 minutes
Cooking time: 10 minutes
Servings: 4

Ingredients:
- 1-pound okra, trimmed
- ½ cup Monterey Jack cheese, shredded
- 1 teaspoon coconut oil, melted
- 1 teaspoon Italian seasonings

Directions:
1. Mix okra with coconut oil and Italian seasonings and put in the air fryer.
2. Cook the vegetables for 8 minutes at 380F.
3. Then shake the vegetables and sprinkle them with cheese.
4. Cook the meal for 2 minutes more.

Nutrition: calories 111, fat 6, fiber 3.6, carbs 8.7, protein 5.7

Pecan Spinach

Preparation time: 5 minutes
Cooking time: 12 minutes
Servings: 4

Ingredients:
- 2 cups fresh spinach, chopped
- 2 pecans, chopped
- 1 tablespoon coconut oil
- ½ teaspoon salt
- ½ teaspoon ground coriander

Directions:
1. Mix spinach with coconut oil, salt, and ground coriander.

2. Put the mixture in the air fryer.
3. Add pecans and cook the meal at 350F for 12 minutes.

Nutrition: calories 82, fat 8.5, fiber 1.1, carbs 1.5, protein 1.2

Okra Salad

Prep time: 15 minutes
Cooking time: 10 minutes
Servings: 4

Ingredients:
- 12 oz okra, chopped
- 1 tablespoon avocado oil
- 1 teaspoon ground turmeric
- 2 oz bacon, chopped, roasted
- 2 cups lettuce, chopped
- 1 tablespoon olive oil
- 1 teaspoon chili flakes

Directions:
1. Mix okra with avocado oil and ground turmeric and put in the air fryer.
2. Cook the okra at 375F for 10 minutes.
3. After this, transfer the okra in the salad bowl, add all remaining ingredients and carefully mix the salad.

Nutrition: calories 151, fat 10.1, fiber 3.2, carbs 8, protein 7.1

Cauliflower Casserole

Preparation time: 10 minutes
Cooking time: 30 minutes
Servings: 4

Ingredients:
- 3 tablespoons coconut oil, melted
- 1 cup heavy cream
- 2 eggs, beaten

- 2 cups Monterey Jack cheese, shredded
- 2 cups cauliflower, chopped
- 1 teaspoon dried cilantro

Directions:
1. Mix cauliflower with coconut oil and put in the air fryer basket in one layer.
2. Then top the vegetables with cilantro and cheese.
3. Then mix heavy cream with eggs and pour the liquid over the cheese.
4. Cook the casserole at 360F for 30 minutes.

Nutrition: calories 446, fat 40.7, fiber 1.3, carbs 4, protein 18.2

Roasted Kabocha Squash

Prep time: 10 minutes
Cooking time: 12 minutes
Servings: 4

Ingredients:
- 10 oz Kabocha squash
- 1 teaspoon onion powder
- 1 oz scallions, chopped
- 1 tablespoon olive oil
- ½ teaspoon chili flakes

Directions:
1. Cut the squash into cubes and sprinkle with onion powder, olive oil, and chili flakes.
2. Put the kabocha squash in the air fryer and cook at 365F for 6 minutes per side.
3. Top the cooked meal with scallions.

Nutrition: calories 119, fat 7, fiber 2.1, carbs 10.7, protein 2.1

Vinegar Cauliflower Mix

Preparation time: 5 minutes
Cooking time: 25 minutes
Servings: 4

Ingredients:
- 1-pound cauliflower, chopped
- 2 oz spring onions, chopped
- ½ teaspoon white pepper
- 4 oz prosciutto, chopped
- 1 pecan, chopped
- 3 tablespoons apple cider vinegar
- 1 tablespoon avocado oil

Directions:
1. Put all ingredients in the air fryer basket and carefully mix.
2. Cook the meal at 360F for 25 minutes.

Nutrition: calories 106, fat 4.7, fiber 3.8, carbs 8.5, protein 8.9

Eggplant Mash

Prep time: 10 minutes
Cooking time: 20 minute
Servings: 6

Ingredients:
- 12 oz eggplants, peeled
- 1 tablespoon coconut oil
- 1 garlic clove, minced
- 1 oz Parmesan, grated
- 1 tablespoon cream cheese

Directions:
1. Chop the eggplants roughly and sprinkle with coconut oil.
2. Put the vegetables in the air fryer and cook at 350F for 20 minutes.
3. Then transfer the cooked eggplants in the blender.
4. Add all remaining ingredients and blend the mixture until smooth.

Nutrition: calories 56, fat 4, fiber 2, carbs 3.7, protein 2.2

Scallions Broccoli

Preparation time: 5 minutes
Cooking time: 15 minutes
Servings: 4

Ingredients:
- 1-pound broccoli, roughly chopped
- 1 tablespoon olive oil
- 1 teaspoon salt
- 2 oz scallions, chopped

Directions:
1. Mix broccoli with olive oil and salt.
2. Put it in the air fryer basket and cook it for 5 minutes per side at 365F.
3. Then sprinkle the broccoli with scallions and cook the meal for 5 minutes more.

Nutrition: calories 73, fat 3.9, fiber 3.3, carbs 8.6, protein 3.4

Cheddar Rutabaga

Prep time: 15 minutes
Cooking time: 8 minute
Servings: 2

Ingredients:
- 6 oz rutabaga, chopped
- 2 oz Cheddar cheese, grated
- 1 tablespoon coconut oil
- ½ teaspoon dried cilantro
- ½ teaspoon salt
- ½ teaspoon onion powder
- 3 tablespoons coconut cream

Directions:
1. Mix rutabaga with coconut oil, dried cilantro, salt, and onion powder.
2. Then add coconut cream and put the vegetables in the air fryer.

3. Cook them at 360F for 4 minutes per side.
4. Top the cooked rutabaga with Cheddar cheese.

Nutrition: calories 257, fat 21.7, fiber 2.7, carbs 9, protein 8.7

Chili Cauliflower

Preparation time: 5 minutes
Cooking time: 15 minutes
Servings: 4

Ingredients:
- 1-pound cauliflower florets
- 2 tablespoons sesame oil
- 2 tablespoons keto hot sauce
- 3 tablespoons lemon juice
- ½ teaspoon white pepper

Directions:
1. Mix sesame oil with lemon juice, hot sauce, and white pepper.
2. Then mix cauliflower florets with the lemon juice mixture and put in the air fryer.
3. Cook them at 360F for 7 minutes per side.
4. Then cook the cauliflower for 1 minute at 400F.

Nutrition: calories 92, fat 7, fiber 3, carbs 6.4, protein 2.4

Coated Jicama

Prep time: 15 minutes
Cooking time: 7 minutes
Servings: 5

Ingredients:
- 15 oz jicama, peeled, cut into sticks
- 1 egg, beaten
- ¼ cup heavy cream

- ½ cup coconut shred
- 1 teaspoon chili powder
- Cooking spray

Directions:
1. Mix egg with heavy cream and chili powder.
2. Dip the jicama sticks in the egg mixture and coat in the coconut shred.
3. Put the coated jicama in the air fryer and spray with cooking spray.
4. Cook the meal at 390F for 7 minutes.

Nutrition: calories 121, fat 8.6, fiber 5.4, carbs 10.2, protein 2.4

Jarlsberg Cauliflower and Broccoli

Preparation time: 5 minutes
Cooking time: 15 minutes
Servings: 4

Ingredients:
- 10 oz broccoli, chopped
- 10 oz cauliflower, chopped
- 4 oz Jarlsberg cheese, grated
- 2 tablespoons apple cider vinegar
- 1 tablespoon avocado oil

Directions:
1. Mix broccoli with cauliflower, apple cider vinegar, and avocado oil.
2. Put the vegetables in the air fryer and top with Jarlsberg cheese.
3. Cook the meal at 365F for 15 minutes.

Nutrition: calories 149, fat 8.8, fiber 3.8, carbs 8.7, protein 10.5

Zucchini Noodles

Prep time: 20 minutes

Cooking time: 5 minute
Servings: 4

Ingredients:
- 3 zucchinis, trimmed
- 1 tablespoon coconut oil
- 1 oz Parmesan, grated

Directions:
1. Spiralize the zucchinis with the help of the spiralizer and mix with coconut oil and Parmesan.
2. Put the mixture in the air fryer and cook at 360F for 5 minutes.
3. Carefully mix the cooked noodles.

Nutrition: calories 76, fat 5.2, fiber 1.6, carbs 5.2, protein 4.1

Broccoli Steaks

Preparation time: 5 minutes
Cooking time: 12 minutes
Servings: 4

Ingredients:
- 2-pound broccoli head
- 1 tablespoon coconut oil, melted
- 1 teaspoon garlic powder
- ½ teaspoon dried oregano

Directions:
1. Slice the broccoli head into steaks.
2. Then rub them with coconut oil, garlic powder, and dried oregano.
3. Put the broccoli steaks in the air fryer and cook them at 365F for 6 minutes per side.

Nutrition: calories 40, fat 3.5, fiber 0.7, carbs 2.1, protein 0.7

Eggplant Slices

Prep time: 15 minutes
Cooking time: 14 minutes
Servings: 2

Ingredients:
- 1 large eggplant, trimmed, peeled
- 1 teaspoon salt
- 1 teaspoon minced garlic
- Cooking spray

Directions:
1. Slice the eggplant and sprinkle with minced garlic, salt, and cooking spray.
2. Then put the eggplant slices in the air fryer and cook them for 7 minutes per side at 350F.

Nutrition: calories 59, fat 0.4, fiber 8.1, carbs 13.9, protein 2.3

Cauliflower Steaks

Preparation time: 10 minutes
Cooking time: 14 minutes
Servings: 4

Ingredients:
- 1.5-pound cauliflower head
- 1 tablespoon sesame oil
- 1 teaspoon ground turmeric
- 1 teaspoon dried dill

Directions:
1. Cut the cauliflower into the steaks and sprinkle with ground turmeric, dill, and sesame oil.
2. Put the steaks in the air fryer and cook at 365F for 7 minutes per side.

Nutrition: calories 75, fat 3.6, fiber 4.4, carbs 9.5, protein 3.5

Garlic Zucchini Slices

Prep time: 10 minutes
Cooking time: 6 minutes
Servings: 4

Ingredients:
- 3 large zucchinis, sliced
- 1 tablespoon minced garlic
- 2 tablespoons sesame oil

Directions:
1. Mix the sesame oil with minced garlic.
2. Then brush the zucchini slices with garlic mixture and put it in the air fryer.
3. Cook them for 3 minutes per side at 400F.

Nutrition: calories 166, fat 7.6, fiber 14.6, carbs 24.9, protein 4.2

Kale Saute

Preparation time: 5 minutes
Cooking time: 10 minutes
Servings: 4

Ingredients:
- 3 cups kale, torn
- 1 cup beef broth
- 1 oz almond, chopped
- ¼ cup mozzarella, shredded
- 1 teaspoon ghee
- 1 teaspoon dried oregano

Directions:
1. Put all ingredients in the air fryer and gently mix with the help of the spoon.
2. Cook the saute at 360F for 10 minutes.

Nutrition: calories 91, fat 5.3, fiber 1.8, carbs 7.3, protein 4.8

Coriander Green Beans

Prep time: 10 minutes
Cooking time: 6 minutes
Servings: 2

Ingredients:
- 12 oz green beans, roughly chopped
- 1 tablespoon ground coriander
- 1 teaspoon salt
- 1 tablespoon coconut oil, melted

Directions:
1. Mix green beans with ground coriander, salt, and coconut oil.
2. Put them in the air fryer and cook for 3 minutes per side and 400F.

Nutrition: calories 111, fat 7, fiber 5.8, carbs 12.2, protein 3.1

Crunchy Kale Leaves

Preparation time: 10 minutes
Cooking time: 12 minutes
Servings: 6

Ingredients:
- 1 egg, beaten
- 1 teaspoon nutritional yeast
- 1 teaspoon sesame oil
- 3 cups kale leaves, roughly chopped

Directions:
1. Sprinkle the kale leaves with sesame oil, nutritional yeast, and egg.
2. Carefully shake the leaves and put in the air fryer.
3. Cook them at 400F for 12 minutes. Shake the leaves every 2 minutes to avoid burning.

Nutrition: calories 36, fat 1.5, fiber 0.6, carbs 3.8, protein 2.2

Vegetable Skewers

Prep time: 15 minutes
Cooking time: 14 minutes
Servings: 4

Ingredients:
- 10 oz halloumi cheese, roughly chopped
- 1 zucchini, roughly chopped
- 1 jalapeno, roughly chopped
- 1 tomato, cut into 4 pieces
- 1 tablespoon olive oil
- ½ teaspoon dried rosemary

Directions:
1. Sting the cheese, zucchini, jalapeno, and tomato into the skewers and sprinkle with olive oil and dried rosemary.
2. Then put the vegetable skewers in the air fryer and cook them at 375F for 14 minutes.

Nutrition: calories 300, fat 24.8, fiber 0.9, carbs 4.4, protein 16.1

Creamy Spinach

Preparation time: 5 minutes
Cooking time: 15 minutes
Servings: 4

Ingredients:
- 3 cups fresh spinach, chopped
- 1 cup heavy cream
- 1 oz macadamia nuts, chopped
- 1 tablespoon butter
- 1 teaspoon salt

Directions:
1. Mix spinach with heavy cream, nuts, butter, and salt.

2. Put the spinach mixture in the ramekin and place the ramekin in the air fryer.
3. Cook the spinach at 350F for 15 minutes.

Nutrition: calories 185, fat 19.4, fiber 1.1, carbs 2.6, protein 1.9

Taco Broccoli Florets

Prep time: 10 minutes
Cooking time: 12 minutes
Servings: 4

Ingredients:
• 1-pound broccoli florets
• 1 tablespoon taco seasonings
• 2 tablespoons olive oil

Directions:
1. Mix broccoli florets with taco seasonings and olive oil.
2. Put the broccoli in the air fryer and cook them at 375F for 12 minutes. Shake the vegetables after 6 minutes of cooking.

Nutrition: calories 106, fat 7.4, fiber 3, carbs 9, protein 3.2

Roasted Olives

Preparation time: 5 minutes
Cooking time: 2 minutes
Servings: 4

Ingredients:
• 8 oz olives, pitted
• 1 teaspoon olive oil

Directions:
1. Sprinkle olives with olive oil and put in the air fryer.

2. Cook them for 2 minutes per side at 400F.

Nutrition: calories 75, fat 7.2, fiber 1.8, carbs 3.6, protein 0.5

Oregano Cauliflower Head

Prep time: 10 minutes
Cooking time: 25 minutes
Servings: 4

Ingredients:
• 16 oz cauliflower head
• 1 tablespoon dried oregano
• 1 tablespoon coconut oil, melted
• 3 eggs, beaten
• 3 tablespoons coconut flour

Directions:
1. Rub the cauliflower head with dried oregano, coconut oil, and coconut flour.
2. Then sprinkle it with eggs and put in the air fryer.
3. Cook the cauliflower head at 365F for 25 minutes.

Nutrition: calories 137, fat 7.5, fiber 5.6, carbs 10.7, protein 7.3

Roasted Mushroom Caps

Preparation time: 5 minutes
Cooking time: 15 minutes
Servings: 4

Ingredients:
• 2-pounds mushroom caps
• 1 tablespoon avocado oil
• 1 teaspoon ground coriander

Directions:

1. Put the mushrooms caps in the air fryer in one layer and sprinkle with avocado oil and ground coriander.
2. Cook the meal at 360F for 15 minutes.

Nutrition: calories 53, fat 1.1, fiber 2.7, carbs 7.7, protein 7.2

Cinnamon Garlic Cloves

Prep time: 5 minutes
Cooking time: 10 minutes
Servings: 4

Ingredients:
• 8 garlic cloves, peeled
• 2 tablespoons olive oil
• ¼ teaspoon dried thyme

Directions:
1. Sprinkle the garlic cloves with olive oil and dried thyme and put in the air fryer.
2. Cook the garlic at 350F for 10 minutes.

Nutrition: calories 69, fat 7, fiber 0.2, carbs 2, protein 0.4

Sautéed Celery Stalks

Preparation time: 5 minutes
Cooking time: 10 minutes
Servings: 4

Ingredients:
• 1-pound celery stalks, chopped
• ½ cup coconut cream
• 1 oz Parmesan, grated
• 1 teaspoon white pepper

Directions:
1. Mix celery stalks with white pepper, Parmesan, and coconut cream.

2. Put the vegetables in the air fryer and cook at 350F for 10 minutes.

Nutrition: calories 111, fat 8.9, fiber 2.6, carbs 5.6, protein 3.8

Keto Buffalo Cauliflower

Prep time: 10 minutes
Cooking time: 6 minutes
Servings: 4

Ingredients:
• 2 cups cauliflower florets
• ¼ cup coconut cream
• 2 tablespoons keto buffalo sauce
• 1 teaspoon olive oil

Directions:
1. Mix cauliflower florets with coconut cream, buffalo sauce, and olive oil.
2. Put them in the air fryer and cook at 400F for 3 minutes per side.

Nutrition: calories 60, fat 4.8, fiber 1.8, carbs 4, protein 1.3

Bacon Brussels Sprouts

Preparation time: 10 minutes
Cooking time: 15 minutes
Servings: 8

Ingredients:
• 1 pound Brussels sprouts, trimmed
• 3 oz bacon, chopped
• 1 tablespoon coconut oil, melted
• 1 teaspoon salt

Directions:
1. Mix Brussel sprouts with coconut oil and salt and put in the air fryer.
2. Top the vegetables with bacon and cook at 360F for 15 minutes. Stir the

vegetables from time to time to avoid burning.

Nutrition: calories 97, fat 6.3, fiber 2.1, carbs 5.3, protein 5.9

Coated Okra

Prep time: 15 minutes
Cooking time: 8 minutes
Servings: 4

Ingredients:
- 1-pound okra, trimmed
- ½ cup coconut flour
- 3 eggs, beaten
- 1 teaspoon chili powder

Directions:
1. Mix coconut flour with chili powder.
2. Then dip the okra in the eggs and coat in the coconut flour mixture.
3. Put the okra in the air fryer and cook at 385F for 4 minutes per side.

Nutrition: calories 155, fat 5.1, fiber 9.9, carbs 19.1, protein 8.4

Roasted Artichoke Hearts

Preparation time: 5 minutes
Cooking time: 15 minutes
Servings: 4

Ingredients:
- 4 artichoke hearts, canned
- 1 teaspoon olive oil
- 1 tablespoon lemon juice
- 1 teaspoon ground black pepper

Directions:
1. Sprinkle the artichoke hearts with olive oil, lemon juice, and ground black pepper.

2. Put them in the air fryer and cook for 15 minutes at 350F.

Nutrition: calories 88, fat 1.5, fiber 8.9, carbs 17.5, protein 5.4

Cajun Eggplants

Prep time: 10 minutes
Cooking time: 15 minutes
Servings: 2

Ingredients:
- 2 eggplants, roughly chopped
- 1 teaspoon Cajun seasonings
- 1 tablespoon sesame oil

Directions:
1. Sprinkle the eggplants with Cajun seasonings and sesame oil.
2. Put the vegetables in the air fryer.
3. Cook them at 360F for 15 minutes.

Nutrition: calories 197, fat 7.8, fiber 19.3, carbs 32.2, protein 5.4

Topped Zucchini

Preparation time: 5 minutes
Cooking time: 12 minutes
Servings: 2

Ingredients:
- 1 large zucchini, trimmed, halved
- 1 teaspoon ground black pepper
- 1 cup Cheddar cheese, shredded
- 1 tablespoon olive oil
- ½ teaspoon dried parsley

Directions:
1. Brush the air fryer basket with olive oil.
2. Put the zucchini inside and sprinkle with ground black pepper.

3. Then top the zucchini with Cheddar cheese and dried parsley.
4. Cook the meal at 375F for 12 minutes.

Nutrition: calories 316, fat 26, fiber 2.1, carbs 6.8, protein 16.1

Egg Green Beans

Prep time: 15 minutes
Cooking time: 5 minutes
Servings: 2

Ingredients:
- 10 oz green beans
- 2 eggs, beaten
- 2 tablespoons coconut shred
- 1 teaspoon ground turmeric
- Cooking spray

Directions:
1. Sprinkle the green beans with eggs and turmeric.
2. Then sprinkle them with coconut shred and put in the air fryer.
3. Spray the green beans with cooking spray and cook at 400F for 5 minutes.

Nutrition: calories 161, fat 9.7, fiber 6.1, carbs 13.2, protein 8.2

Roasted Artichoke

Preparation time: 5 minutes
Cooking time: 15 minutes
Servings: 2

Ingredients:
- 2 artichokes, trimmed
- 1 tablespoon olive oil
- 1 teaspoon onion powder

Directions:

1. Put artichokes in the air fryer and sprinkle with onion powder and olive oil.
2. Cook the artichokes at 355F for 15 minutes.

Nutrition: calories 140, fat 7.3, fiber 8.8, carbs 18, protein 5.4

Cajun Okra

Prep time: 10 minutes
Cooking time: 10 minutes
Servings: 3

Ingredients:
- 12 oz okra, chopped
- 1 teaspoon Cajun seasonings
- 1 tablespoon sesame oil

Directions:
1. Mix okra with Cajun seasonings and sesame oil.
2. Put the vegetables in the air fryer and cook at 360F for 5 minutes.
3. Then shake the vegetables and cook them for 5 minutes more.

Nutrition: calories 85, fat 4.8, fiber 3.6, carbs 8.5, protein 2.2

Marinated Bell Peppers

Preparation time: 10 minutes
Cooking time: 5 minutes
Servings: 4

Ingredients:
- 4 bell peppers, trimmed
- 1 tablespoon olive oil
- 1 teaspoon minced garlic
- 1 tablespoon apple cider vinegar

Directions:
1. Sprinkle the bell peppers with olive oil and put in the air fryer.

2. Cook the bell peppers at 400F for 5 minutes.
3. Then chop the bell peppers roughly and sprinkle with minced garlic and apple cider vinegar.

Nutrition: calories 70, fat 3.8, fiber 1.6, carbs 9.3, protein 1.2

Roasted Avocado Wedges

Prep time: 10 minutes
Cooking time: 6 minutes
Servings: 4

Ingredients:
- 1 avocado, pitted, cut into 4 wedges
- 4 teaspoons coconut shred
- 1 egg, beaten
- ½ teaspoon ground nutmeg

Directions:
1. Dip the avocado wedges in the egg and sprinkle with ground nutmeg.
2. Then sprinkle the avocado with coconut shred and put it in the air fryer.
3. Cook the meal at 400F for 3 minutes per side.

Nutrition: calories 136, fat 12.7, fiber 3.8, carbs 5.2, protein 2.4

Herbed Kalamata Olives

Preparation time: 5 minutes
Cooking time: 8 minutes
Servings: 4

Ingredients:
- 8 Kalamata Olives, pitted
- 1 teaspoon Italian seasonings
- 1 tablespoon olive oil
- 1 teaspoon coconut aminos

Directions:
1. Sprinkle olives with Italian seasonings, olive oil, and coconut aminos.
2. Put the olives in the air fryer and cook at 360F for 8 minutes.

Nutrition: calories 45, fat 4.8, fiber 0.3, carbs 0.9, protein 0.1

Cauliflower Balls

Prep time: 15 minutes
Cooking time: 12 minutes
Servings: 4

Ingredients:
- 2 cups cauliflower, shredded
- 3 tablespoons coconut flour
- 1 teaspoon ground cumin
- 2 tablespoons coconut oil
- 1 egg, beaten
- 1 teaspoon salt
- 1 teaspoon ground coriander
- 1 teaspoon dried basil
- Cooking spray

Directions:
1. Mix shredded cauliflower with coconut flour, ground cumin, coconut oil, egg, salt, ground coriander, and dried basil.
2. Make the balls from the mixture and put it in the air fryer.
3. Spray the cauliflower balls with cooking spray and cook them at 385F for 6 minutes per side or until they are golden brown.

Nutrition: calories 134, fat 9.6, fiber 5.1, carbs 9, protein 4

Greek Style Olives

Preparation time: 5 minutes

Cooking time: 12 minutes
Servings: 4

Ingredients:
- 6 oz Feta cheese, crumbled
- 8 oz black olives, pitted
- 1 tablespoon coconut oil, melted
- 1 teaspoon dried thyme

Directions:
1. Put olives in the air fryer and sprinkle with coconut oil and dried thyme.
2. Cook them at 350F for 12 minutes.
3. Sprinkle the cooked olives with crumbled Feta cheese.

Nutrition: calories 207, fat 18.5, fiber 1.9, carbs 5.5, protein 6.5

Zucchini Patties

Prep time: 15 minutes
Cooking time: 8 minutes
Servings: 4

Ingredients:
- 2 zucchinis, grated
- 1 tablespoon dried dill
- 1 teaspoon cream cheese
- 1 cup almond flour
- 1 teaspoon salt
- Cooking spray

Directions:
1. Mix zucchini with dried dill, cream cheese, almond flour, and salt
2. Make the patties from the zucchini mixture and put it in the air fryer.
3. Sprinkle the patties with cooking spray and cook at 375F for 4 minutes per side.

Nutrition: calories 189, fat 13.8, fiber 4.2, carbs 9.7, protein 7.4

Brussel Sprouts Roast

Preparation time: 5 minutes
Cooking time: 12 minutes
Servings: 4

Ingredients:
- 1-pound Brussel sprouts, halved
- 1 tablespoon olive oil
- 1 teaspoon dried dill
- 2 oz Feta, crumbled

Directions:
1. Mix Brussel sprouts with olive oil and dried dill.
2. Put the vegetables in the air fryer and cook at 375F for 6 minutes per side.
3. Top the cooked vegetables with crumbled feta.

Nutrition: calories 117, fat 6.9, fiber 4.3, carbs 11, protein 5.9

Broccoli Rice Balls

Prep time: 15 minutes
Cooking time: 5 minute
Servings: 2

Ingredients:
- 1 cup broccoli, shredded
- 3 oz Feta, crumbled
- 1 egg, beaten
- 1 tablespoon almond flour
- ½ teaspoon white pepper
- 1 teaspoon mascarpone
- 1 teaspoon avocado oil

Directions:
1. Brush the air fryer basket with avocado oil.
2. Then mix all remaining ingredients and make the balls.

3. Put the balls in the air fryer in one layer and cook at 400F for 5 minutes.

Nutrition: calories 189, fat 13.7, fiber 1.8, carbs 6.2, protein 11.2

Cabbage Fritters

Preparation time: 10 minutes
Cooking time: 12 minutes
Servings: 4

Ingredients:
- 1 cup white cabbage, shredded
- 3 eggs, beaten
- 1 oz scallions, chopped
- 1/3 cup coconut flour
- 1 teaspoon cream cheese
- Cooking spray

Directions:
1. Spray the air fryer basket with cooking spray from inside.
2. Then mix all remaining ingredients in the bowl.
3. Make the fritters from the cabbage mixture and put in the air fryer basket in one layer.
4. Cook the fritters at 375F for 6 minutes per side.

Nutrition: calories 97, fat 4.6, fiber 4.6, carbs 8.5, protein 5.9

Broccoli Gnocchi

Prep time: 15 minutes
Cooking time: 4 minutes
Servings: 4

Ingredients:
- 2 cups broccoli, chopped, boiled
- 2 oz provolone cheese, grated
- 1 egg, beaten
- 1 teaspoon white pepper
- 1 teaspoon mascarpone
- 3 tablespoons almond flour
- 1 tablespoon coconut oil
- 1 teaspoon dried parsley

Directions:
1. Mix all ingredients in the mixing bowl until smooth.
2. Then make the gnocchi and put them in the air fryer in one layer.
3. Cook the gnocchi at 400F for 2 minutes per side.

Nutrition: calories 146, fat 11.1, fiber 1.9, carbs 4.9, protein 7.6

Lemon Peppers

Preparation time: 5 minutes
Cooking time: 15 minutes
Servings: 4

Ingredients:
- 2 cups bell peppers, roughly chopped
- 2 tablespoons lemon juice
- 1 teaspoon butter, softened
- 1 garlic clove, diced
- 1 teaspoon ground clove

Directions:
1. Put the bell peppers in the air fryer basket and sprinkle with butter, garlic clove, and ground clove.
2. Cook the bell peppers for 15 minutes at 350F. Stir the peppers every 5 minutes to avoid burning.
3. Then transfer the cooked peppers in the bowl and sprinkle with lemon juice.

Nutrition: calories 32, fat 1.3, fiber 1, carbs 5.2, protein 0.8

Portobello Steak

Prep time: 10 minutes
Cooking time: 5 minute
Servings: 4

Ingredients:
- 1-pound Portobello mushrooms
- 1 teaspoon ground coriander
- 4 teaspoons butter
- ½ teaspoon salt

Directions:
1. Sprinkle the mushrooms with ground coriander, salt, and butter.
2. Put the mushrooms in the air fryer and cook for 5 minutes at 400F.

Nutrition: calories 61, fat 3.8, fiber 1.4, carbs 4.1, protein 4.1

Dessert

Coconut Muffins

Preparation time: 5 minutes
Cooking time: 25 minutes
Servings: 5

Ingredients:
- ½ cup coconut flour
- 2 tablespoons cocoa powder
- 3 tablespoons Erythritol
- 1 teaspoon baking powder
- 2 tablespoons coconut oil
- 2 eggs, beaten
- ½ cup coconut shred

Directions:
1. In the mixing bowl, mix all ingredients.
2. Then pour the mixture in the molds of the muffin and transfer in the air fryer basket.
3. Cook the muffins at 350F for 25 minutes.

Nutrition: calories 206, fat 16.7, fiber 7.1, carbs 13, protein 4.2

Coffee Muffins

Prep time: 10 minutes
Cooking time: 11 minutes
Servings: 6

Ingredients:
- 1 cup coconut flour
- 4 tablespoons coconut oil
- 1 teaspoon vanilla extract
- 1 teaspoon instant coffee
- 1 teaspoon baking powder
- 1 egg, beaten
- ¼ cup Erythritol

Directions:

1. Mix coconut flour with coconut oil, vanilla extract, instant coffee, baking powder, egg, and Erythritol.
2. Put the mixture in the muffin molds and cook in the air fryer at 375F for 11 minutes.

Nutrition: calories 172, fat 11.8, fiber 8, carbs 13.9, protein 3.6

Almond Cookies

Preparation time: 5 minutes
Cooking time: 15 minutes
Servings: 8

Ingredients:
- 1 cup almond flour
- 2 oz almonds, grinded
- 2 tablespoons Erythritol
- ½ teaspoon baking powder
- 5 tablespoons coconut oil, softened
- ½ teaspoon vanilla extract

Directions:
1. Mix almond flour with almonds, Erythritol, baking powder, coconut oil, and vanilla extract. Knead the dough.
2. Make the small cookies and place them in the air fryer basket.
3. Cook the cookies at 350F for 15 minutes.

Nutrition: calories 199, fat 18.7, fiber 2.4, carbs 4.7, protein 4.5

Thumbprint Cookies

Prep time: 15 minutes
Cooking time: 9 minutes
Servings: 6

Ingredients:
- 2 teaspoons coconut oil, softened

- 1 tablespoon Erythritol
- 1 egg, beaten
- ½ cup coconut flour
- 1 oz almonds, chopped

Directions:
1. Mix all ingredients in the mixing bowl. Knead the dough.
2. Then make cookies from the dough and put in the air fryer basket.
3. Cook the cookies at 365F for 9 minutes.

Nutrition: calories 91, fat 5.6, fiber 4.6, carbs 10.2, protein 3.3

Pecan Bars

Preparation time: 5 minutes
Cooking time: 40 minutes
Servings: 12

Ingredients:
- 2 cups coconut flour
- 5 tablespoons Erythritol
- 4 tablespoons coconut oil, softened
- ½ cup heavy cream
- 1 egg, beaten
- 4 pecans, chopped

Directions:
1. Mix coconut flour, Erythritol, coconut oil, heavy cream, and egg.
2. Pour the batter in the air fryer basket and flatten well.
3. Top the mixture with pecans and cook the meal at 350F for 40 minutes.
4. Cut the cooked meal into the bars.

Nutrition: calories 174, fat 12.1, fiber 8.5, carbs 14.2, protein 3.7

Brown Muffins

Prep time: 15 minutes

Cooking time: 10 minutes
Servings: 2

Ingredients:
- 1 egg, beaten
- 1 tablespoon coconut oil, softened
- 2 tablespoons almond flour
- 1 tablespoon cocoa powder
- 1 tablespoon Erythritol
- 1 teaspoon ground cinnamon

Directions:
1. Mix egg with coconut oil, almond flour, cocoa powder, Erythritol, and ground cinnamon.
2. Pour the muffin batter in the muffin molds.
3. Bake the muffins at 375F for 10 minutes.

Nutrition: calories 141, fat 12.7, fiber 2.2, carbs 4.1, protein 4.8

Lime Bars

Preparation time: 10 minutes
Cooking time: 35 minutes
Servings: 10

Ingredients:
- 3 tablespoons coconut oil, melted
- 3 tablespoons Splenda
- 1 ½ cup coconut flour
- 3 eggs, beaten
- 1 teaspoon lime zest, grated
- 3 tablespoons lime juice

Directions:
1. Cover the air fryer basket bottom with baking paper.
2. Then in the mixing bowl, mix Splenda with coconut flour, eggs, lime zest, and lime juice.
3. Pour the mixture in the air fryer basket and flatten gently.

4. Cook the meal at 350F for 35 minutes.
5. Then cool the cooked meal little and cut into bars.

Nutrition: calories 144, fat 7.2, fiber 7.2, carbs 15.7, protein 4.1

Tender Macadamia Bars

Prep time: 15 minutes
Cooking time: 30 minutes
Servings: 10

Ingredients:
- 3 tablespoons butter, softened
- 1 teaspoon baking powder
- 1 teaspoon apple cider vinegar
- 1.5 cup coconut flour
- 3 tablespoons swerve
- 1 teaspoon vanilla extract
- 2 eggs, beaten
- 2 oz macadamia nuts, chopped
- Cooking spray

Directions:
1. Spray the air fryer basket with cooking spray.
2. Then mix all remaining ingredients in the mixing bowl and stir until you get a homogenous mixture.
3. Pour the mixture in the air fryer basket and cook at 345F for 30 minutes.
4. When the mixture is cooked, cut it into bars and transfer in the serving plates.

Nutrition: calories 158, fat 10.4, fiber 7.7, carbs 13.1, protein 4

Cinnamon Zucchini Bread

Preparation time: 10 minutes
Cooking time: 40 minutes

Servings: 12

Ingredients:
- 2 cups coconut flour
- 2 teaspoons baking powder
- ¾ cup Erythritol
- ½ cup coconut oil, melted
- 1 teaspoon apple cider vinegar
- 1 teaspoon vanilla extract
- 3 eggs, beaten
- 1 zucchini, grated
- 1 teaspoon ground cinnamon

Directions:
1. In the mixing bowl, mix coconut flour with baking powder, Erythritol, coconut oil, apple cider vinegar, vanilla extract, eggs, zucchini, and ground cinnamon.
2. Transfer the mixture in the air fryer basket and flatten it in the shape of the bread.
3. Cook the bread at 350F for 40 minutes.

Nutrition: calories 179, fat 12.2, fiber 8.3, carbs 14.6, protein 4.3

Poppy Seeds Muffins

Prep time: 10 minutes
Cooking time: 10 minutes
Servings: 5

Ingredients:
- 5 tablespoons coconut oil, softened
- 1 egg, beaten
- 1 teaspoon vanilla extract
- 1 tablespoon poppy seeds
- 1 teaspoon baking powder
- 2 tablespoons Erythritol
- 1 cup coconut flour

Directions:
1. In the mixing bowl, mix coconut oil with egg, vanilla extract, poppy seeds,

baking powder, Erythritol, and coconut flour.

2. When the mixture is homogenous, pour it in the muffin molds and transfer it in the air fryer basket.

3. Cook the muffins for 10 minutes at 365F.

Nutrition: calories 239, fat 17.7, fiber 9.8, carbs 17.1, protein 4.6

Almond Pie

Preparation time: 10 minutes
Cooking time: 35 minutes
Servings: 8

Ingredients:
- 2 eggs, beaten
- ¾ cup Erythritol
- ¼ cup almond flour
- 2 tablespoons coconut oil, melted
- 1 teaspoon lime zest, grated
- 1 teaspoon baking powder
- 1 teaspoon vanilla extract
- ½ teaspoon apple cider vinegar
- 1 oz almonds, chopped

Directions:
1. Mix all ingredients in the mixing bowl and whisk until smooth.
2. Then pour the mixture in the baking pan and flatten gently.
3. Put the baking pan in the air fryer and cook the pie at 365F for 35 minutes.

Nutrition: calories 89, fat 7.9, fiber 0.9, carbs 2, protein 2

Vanilla Scones

Prep time: 20 minutes
Cooking time: 10 minutes
Servings: 6

Ingredients:
- 4 oz coconut flour
- ½ teaspoon baking powder
- 1 teaspoon apple cider vinegar
- 2 teaspoons mascarpone
- ¼ cup heavy cream
- 1 teaspoon vanilla extract
- 1 tablespoon Erythritol
- Cooking spray

Directions:
1. In the mixing bowl, mix coconut flour with baking powder, apple cider vinegar, mascarpone, heavy cream, vanilla extract, and Erythritol.
2. Knead the dough and cut into scones.
3. Then put them in the air fryer basket and sprinkle with cooking spray.
4. Cook the vanilla scones at 365F for 10 minutes.

Nutrition: calories 104, fat 4.1, fiber 8.1, carbs 14, protein 3

Raspberry Tart

Preparation time: 5 minutes
Cooking time: 20 minutes
Servings: 8

Ingredients:
- 5 egg whites
- 1/3 cup Erythritol
- 1.5 cup coconut flour
- 1 teaspoon lime zest, grated
- 1 teaspoon baking powder
- 1/3 cup coconut oil, melted
- 3 oz raspberries
- Cooking spray

Directions:

1. Mix eggs with Erythritol, coconut flour, lime zest, baking powder, and coconut oil.
2. Whisk the mixture until smooth.
3. Then spray the air fryer basket with cooking spray and pour the batter inside.
4. Top the batter with raspberries and cook at 360F for 20 minutes.

Nutrition: calories 96, fat 9.2, fiber 0.8, carbs 1.9, protein 2.4

Vanilla Pie

Prep time: 10 minutes
Cooking time: 40 minutes
Servings: 8

Ingredients:
- ½ cup coconut cream
- 3 eggs, beaten
- 1 tablespoon vanilla extract
- 1 teaspoon baking powder
- 3 tablespoons swerve
- 1 cup coconut flour
- 1 tablespoon coconut oil, melted

Directions:
1. Mix coconut cream with eggs, vanilla extract, baking powder, swerve, coconut flour, and coconut oil.
2. Then transfer the mixture in the air fryer basket and flatten it gently.
3. Cook the pie at 355F for 40 minutes.

Nutrition: calories 139, fat 8.9, fiber 5.3, carbs 9.5, protein 4.4

Almond Donuts

Preparation time: 15 minutes
Cooking time: 14 minutes
Servings: 6

Ingredients:
- 8 ounces almond flour
- 2 tablespoons Erythritol
- 1 egg, beaten
- 2 tablespoons almond butter, softened
- 4 ounces heavy cream
- 1 teaspoon baking powder

Directions:
1. In the mixing bowl, mix almond flour, Erythritol, egg, almond butter, heavy cream, and baking powder. Knead the dough.
2. Roll up the dough and make the donuts with the help of the cutter.
3. Put the donuts in the air fryer basket and cook at 365F for 7 minutes per side.

Nutrition: calories 323, fat 29.4, fiber 4.6, carbs 10, protein 10.5

Nutmeg Donuts

Prep time: 20 minutes
Cooking time: 6 minutes
Servings: 4

Ingredients:
- 1 teaspoon ground nutmeg
- ½ teaspoon baking powder
- ½ cup almond flour
- 1 tablespoon Swerve
- 1 egg, beaten
- 1 tablespoon coconut oil, softened
- Cooking spray

Directions:
1. Spray the air fryer basket with cooking spray from inside.
2. Then mix all remaining ingredients and knead the dough.
3. Make the donuts from the dough and put them in the air fryer.

4. Cook the donuts at 390F for 3 minutes per side.

Nutrition: calories 69, fat 6.4, fiber 0.5, carbs 1.4, protein 2.2

Soft Turmeric Cookies

Preparation time: 10 minutes
Cooking time: 20 minutes
Servings: 12

Ingredients:
- 2 eggs, beaten
- 1 tablespoon coconut cream
- 3 tablespoons coconut oil, melted
- 2 teaspoons ground turmeric
- 1 teaspoon vanilla extract
- 2.5 cup coconut flour
- 2 tablespoons Erythritol

Directions:
1. Mix all ingredients in the mixing bowl.
2. Knead the dough and make the cookies using the cutter.
3. Put the cookies in the air fryer basket and cook at 350F for 20 minutes.

Nutrition: calories 147, fat 17, fiber 10.1, carbs 17.6, protein 4.3

Mint Pie

Prep time: 15 minutes
Cooking time: 25 minutes
Servings: 2

Ingredients:
- 1 tablespoon instant coffee
- 2 tablespoons almond butter, softened
- 2 tablespoons Erythritol
- 1 teaspoon dried mint
- 3 eggs, beaten
- 1 teaspoon spearmint, dried
- 4 teaspoons coconut flour
- Cooking spray

Directions:
1. Spray the air fryer basket with cooking spray.
2. Then mix all ingredients in the mixer bowl.
3. When you get a smooth mixture, transfer it in the air fryer basket. Flatten it gently.
4. Cook the pie at 365F for 25 minutes.

Nutrition: calories 313, fat 19.6, fiber 11.7, carbs 19.6, protein 15.7

Saffron Cookies

Preparation time: 10 minutes
Cooking time: 15 minutes
Servings: 12

Ingredients:
- 2 cups coconut flour
- ½ cup Erythritol
- ¼ cup coconut, melted
- 1 egg, beaten
- 2 teaspoons saffron
- 1 teaspoon vanilla extract

Directions:
1. Mix all ingredients in the bowl and knead the dough.
2. Make the cookies and put them in the air fryer basket in one layer.
3. Cook the cookies at 355F for 15 minutes.

Nutrition: calories 106, fat 4.3, fiber 8.2, carbs 12.4, protein 4.5

Keto Balls

Prep time: 15 minutes
Cooking time: 4 minutes
Servings: 10

Ingredients:
- 2 eggs, beaten
- 1 teaspoon coconut oil, melted
- 9 oz coconut flour
- 5 oz provolone cheese, shredded
- 2 tablespoons Erythritol
- 1 teaspoon baking powder
- ¼ teaspoon ground coriander
- Cooking spray

Directions:
1. Mix eggs with coconut oil, coconut flour, Provolone cheese, Erythritol, baking powder, and ground cinnamon.
2. Make the balls and put them in the air fryer basket.
3. Sprinkle the balls with cooking spray and cook at 400F for 4 minutes.

Nutrition: calories 176, fat 7.8, fiber 10.9, carbs 18.9, protein 8.4

Sage Muffins

Preparation time: 10 minutes
Cooking time: 20 minutes
Servings: 8

Ingredients:
- 3 tablespoons coconut oil, softened
- 1 egg, beaten
- ½ cup Erythritol
- ¼ cup almond flour
- 1 teaspoon dried sage
- 3 tablespoons mascarpone
- ½ teaspoon baking soda
- Cooking spray

Directions:
1. Spray the muffin molds with cooking spray.
2. Then mix all ingredients in the mixing bowl and stir until smooth.
3. Pour the mixture in the muffin molds and transfer in the air fryer.
4. Cook the muffins at 350F for 20 minutes.

Nutrition: calories 85, fat 8.3, fiber 0.4, carbs 0.9, protein 1.4

Pecan Tarts

Prep time: 10 minutes
Cooking time: 10 minutes
Servings: 5

Ingredients:
- 3 pecans, chopped
- ½ cup coconut flour
- 1 egg, beaten
- 1 tablespoon coconut oil, softened
- 1 tablespoon swerve
- ½ teaspoon baking powder
- Cooking spray

Directions:
1. Spray the air fryer basket with cooking spray.
2. Then mix coconut flour with egg, coconut oil, swerve, and baking powder.
3. When you get a smooth batter, pour it in the air fryer basket, flatten gently, and top with pecans.
4. Cook the tart at 375F for 10 minutes.

Nutrition: calories 143, fat 10.8, fiber 5.7, carbs 9.5, protein 3.6

Raspberry Jam

Preparation time: 10 minutes

Cooking time: 20 minutes
Servings: 12

Ingredients:
- ¼ cup Erythritol
- 7 oz raspberries
- 1 tablespoon lime juice
- ¼ cup of water

Directions:
1. Put all ingredients in the air fryer and stir gently.
2. Cook the jam at 350F for 20 minutes. Stir the jam every 5 minutes to avoid burning.

Nutrition: calories 9, fat 0.1, fiber 1.1, carbs 2, protein 0.2

Vanilla Shortcake

Prep time: 15 minutes
Cooking time: 30 minutes
Servings: 4

Ingredients:
- 3 eggs, beaten
- ½ cup almond flour
- ½ teaspoon baking powder
- 2 teaspoons swerve
- 1 teaspoon vanilla extract
- ½ cup coconut cream
- Cooking spray

Directions:
1. Spray the air fryer basket with cooking spray.
2. Then mix eggs with almond flour, baking powder, swerve, vanilla extract, and coconut cream.
3. When the mixture is smooth, pour it in the air fryer basket and flatten gently with the help of the spatula.
4. Cook the shortcake at 355F for 30 minutes.

Nutrition: calories 140, fat 12.2, fiber 1.1, carbs 3.1, protein 5.6

Raspberry Cream

Preparation time: 10 minutes
Cooking time: 20 minutes
Servings: 6

Ingredients:
- ½ cup raspberries
- 1 tablespoon lime juice
- 2 tablespoons water
- 3 tablespoons Erythritol
- ¼ teaspoon ground cinnamon

Directions:
1. Blend the raspberries and mix with lime juice, water, Erythritol, and ground cinnamon.
2. Pour the mixture in the air fryer and cook at 345F for 20 minutes.

Nutrition: calories 6, fat 0.1, fiber 0.7, carbs 1.5, protein 0.1

Coconut Hand Pies

Prep time: 20 minutes
Cooking time: 26 minutes
Servings: 6

Ingredients:
- 8 oz coconut flour
- 1 teaspoon vanilla extract
- 2 tablespoons Swerve
- 2 eggs, beaten
- 1 tablespoon almond butter, melted
- 1 tablespoon almond meal
- 2 tablespoons coconut shred
- Cooking spray

Directions:

1. Mix coconut flour with vanilla extract, Swerve, eggs, almond butter, and almond meal.
2. Knead the dough and roll it up.
3. Cut the dough into squares and sprinkle with coconut shred.
4. Fold the squares into the shape of pies and put in the air fryer basket.
5. Sprinkle the pies with cooking spray and cook at 345F for 13 minutes per side.

Nutrition: calories 128, fat 6.5, fiber 7.1, carbs 11.7, protein 5.1

Milk Pie

Preparation time: 10 minutes
Cooking time: 20 minutes
Servings: 8

Ingredients:
- 2 egg, beaten
- 3 tablespoons Erythritol
- 3 tablespoons butter, melted
- ¼ cup organic almond milk
- 4 tablespoons coconut flour
- ½ teaspoon baking powder

Directions:
1. Put all ingredients in the mixer bowl and blend until smooth.
2. Pour the mixture in the air fryer basket and cook at 365F for 20 minutes.

Nutrition: calories 73, fat 6.1, fiber 1.3, carbs 2.6, protein 2.2

Keto Hot Chocolate

Prep time: 10 minutes
Cooking time: 7 minutes
Servings: 3

Ingredients:
- ¼ teaspoon vanilla extract
- 2 cups organic almond milk
- 1 teaspoon coconut oil
- 1 tablespoon cocoa powder
- 2 tablespoons Erythritol

Directions:
1. Mix all ingredients in the air fryer basket.
2. Stir the mixture until smooth.
3. Cook the dessert at 375F for 7 minutes.

Nutrition: calories 386, fat 39.9, fiber 4.1, carbs 9.9, protein 4

Cocoa Chia Pudding

Preparation time: 40 minutes
Cooking time: 10 minutes
Servings: 3

Ingredients:
- 3 tablespoons chia seeds
- 2 cups coconut cream
- 1 teaspoon of cocoa powder
- 1 teaspoon vanilla extract
- 1 tablespoon Erythritol

Directions:
1. Pour the coconut cream in the air fryer.
2. Add cocoa powder, vanilla extract, and Erythritol. Stir the liquid until smooth.
3. Then cook it at 350F for 10 minutes.
4. Add chia seeds, carefully mix the dessert, and leave it to rest for 40 minutes.

Nutrition: calories 442, fat 42.6, fiber 8.6, carbs 15.3, protein 6.1

Pumpkin Spices Muffins

Prep time: 15 minutes
Cooking time: 10 minutes
Servings: 6

Ingredients:
- 1 cup coconut flour
- 1 tablespoon pumpkin spices
- ½ teaspoon baking powder
- 2 eggs, beaten
- 2 tablespoons coconut oil
- 2 tablespoons Erythritol
- 1 tablespoon coconut cream

Directions:
1. Mix all ingredients in the mixing bowl.
2. When the batter is smooth, pour it in the muffin molds and transfer in the air fryer basket.
3. Cook the muffins at 365F for 10 minutes.

Nutrition: calories 149, fat 8.7, fiber 8.2, carbs 14.4, protein 4.6

Egg Custard

Preparation time: 5 minutes
Cooking time: 30 minutes
Servings: 6

Ingredients:
- 6 eggs, beaten
- 2 cups heavy cream
- ½ cup Erythritol
- 1 teaspoon vanilla extract

Directions:
1. Whisk all ingredients until smooth and pour in the air fryer basket.
2. Cook the custard at 345F for 30 minutes.
3. Then cool it well.

Nutrition: calories 203, fat 19.2, fiber 0 carbs 1.6, protein 6.4

Butter Cookies

Prep time: 15 minutes
Cooking time: 10 minutes
Servings: 5

Ingredients:
- 4 tablespoons butter, softened
- 4 teaspoons Splenda
- 1 egg, beaten
- 1 cup coconut flour

Directions:
1. In the mixing bowl, mix butter, Splenda, egg, and coconut flour.
2. Knead the dough and make the balls (cookies).
3. Put them in the air fryer and cook at 365F for 10 minutes.

Nutrition: calories 206, fat 12.5, fiber 9.6, carbs 19.3, protein 4.4

Mascarpone Brownies

Preparation time: 10 minutes
Cooking time: 25 minutes
Servings: 6

Ingredients:
- 6 tablespoons mascarpone
- 3 eggs, beaten
- 2 tablespoons cocoa powder
- 3 tablespoons butter, softened
- 1 cup almond flour
- ¼ teaspoon baking soda
- ¼ cup coconut cream
- 3 tablespoons Erythritol

Directions:

1. Mix all ingredients in the mixing bowl until smooth.
2. Then line the air fryer basket with baking paper and pour the brownie batter inside.
3. Cook the meal at 360F for 25 minutes.
4. Then cool the dessert little and cut into brownies.

Nutrition: calories 248, fat 21.5, fiber 2.8, carbs 6.2, protein 9.1

Chia Balls

Prep time: 15 minutes
Cooking time: 10 minutes
Servings: 4

Ingredients:
- 4 teaspoons chia seeds
- 1 tablespoon coconut oil, softened
- 1 tablespoon Erythritol
- ½ teaspoon vanilla extract
- 1 tablespoon almond flour
- 1 teaspoon almond flakes
- 1 egg, beaten
- Cooking spray

Directions:
1. Spray the air fryer basket with cooking spray.
2. Then mix all remaining ingredients in the mixing bowl and stir until homogenous.
3. Make the balls from the mixture and put in the air fryer in one layer.
4. Cook the chia balls at 365F for 10 minutes.

Nutrition: calories 126, fat 9.7, fiber 5.1, carbs 10.2, protein 4.1

Avocado Cream

Preparation time: 10 minutes
Cooking time: 30 minutes
Servings: 5

Ingredients:
- 1 avocado, peeled, pitted, chopped
- 1 egg, beaten
- 2 tablespoon Erythritol
- 1 cup coconut cream
- 1 tablespoon butter, softened
- ½ teaspoon ground nutmeg

Directions:
1. Blend the avocado with egg, Erythritol, coconut cream, butter, and ground nutmeg.
2. When the liquid is smooth, transfer it in the ramekins.
3. Put the ramekins in the air fryer basket and cook at 345F for 30 minutes.

Nutrition: calories 227, fat 22.5, fiber 3.8, carbs 6.3, protein 3

Cream Cheese Bombs

Prep time: 10 minutes
Cooking time: 5 minutes
Servings: 2

Ingredients:
- 2 tablespoons cream cheese
- 4 tablespoons coconut flour
- 1 teaspoon vanilla extract
- 1 egg, beaten
- 1 tablespoon Erythritol
- 2 tablespoons coconut shred

Directions:
1. Mix cream cheese with coconut flour, vanilla extract, egg, Erythritol, and coconut shred.
2. Make the balls from the mixture and put in the air fryer basket.

3. Cook the cheese bombs at 390F for 5 minutes.

Nutrition: calories 166, fat 10.5, fiber 6.7, carbs 12, protein 5.9

Coconut Cream Cups

Preparation time: 5 minutes
Cooking time: 10 minutes
Servings: 2

Ingredients:
- 1 cup coconut cream
- 4 egg yolks
- 2 tablespoons Erythritol
- 1 tablespoon coconut flour
- 1 teaspoon vanilla extract

Directions:
1. Whisk the egg yolks with coconut cream and Erythritol.
2. Then add coconut flour and vanilla extract. Whisk the mixture until smooth.
3. Pour the mixture in the baking cups and put it in the air fryer basket.
4. Cook the cups at 390F for 10 minutes.

Nutrition: calories 105, fat 3.8, fiber 4.1, carbs 10.6, protein 8.6

Lemon Custard

Prep time: 10 minutes
Cooking time: 35 minutes
Servings: 2

Ingredients:
- ½ cup heavy cream
- 1 teaspoon lemon zest, grated
- 1 teaspoon vanilla extract
- 1 tablespoon butter, softened
- 3 eggs, beaten

Directions:
1. Whisk all ingredients in the mixing bowl until smooth.
2. Pour the mixture in the baking pan and transfer in the air fryer basket.
3. Cook the custard at 340F for 35 minutes.

Nutrition: calories 255, fat 23.4, fiber 0.1, carbs 1.8, protein 9

Sweet Cream Cheese Zucchini

Preparation time: 10 minutes
Cooking time: 15 minutes
Servings: 4

Ingredients:
- 4 teaspoons cream cheese
- 1 zucchini, grated
- 2 tablespoons Erythritol
- ¼ cup heavy cream
- 1 teaspoon butter

Directions:
1. Mix cream cheese with grated zucchini, heavy cream, butter, and Erythritol.
2. Put the mixture in the air fryer basket and flatten gently.
3. Cook the meal at 360F for 15 minutes.

Nutrition: calories 54, fat 5, fiber 0.5, carbs 1.9, protein 1

Sesame Seeds Cookies

Prep time: 15 minutes
Cooking time: 10 minutes
Servings: 8

Ingredients:
- 1 cup almond flour

- 2 tablespoons coconut shred
- 2 eggs, beaten
- 1 teaspoon baking powder
- ¼ cup Splenda
- 3 tablespoons sesame seeds
- 1 tablespoon coconut oil, softened

Directions:
1. Put all ingredients in the mixing bowl and knead the dough.
2. Make the balls from the dough and press them gently in the shape of the cookies.
3. Put the cookies in the air fryer basket in one layer and cook them for 10 minutes at 360F.

Nutrition: calories 177, fat 12.4, fiber 2.2, carbs 10.7, protein 5

Walnut Bars

Preparation time: 15 minutes
Cooking time: 16 minutes
Servings: 4

Ingredients:
- 1 egg, beaten
- 2 tablespoons Erythritol
- 7 tablespoons coconut oil, softened
- 1 teaspoon vanilla extract
- ¼ cup coconut flour
- 1 oz walnuts, chopped
- ½ teaspoon baking powder

Directions:
1. Mix egg with Erythritol, coconut oil, vanilla extract, coconut flour, and baking powder.
2. Stir the mixture gently, add walnuts, and mix the mixture until homogenous.
3. Pour the mixture in the air fryer basket and flatten gently.

4. Cook the walnut bars at 375F for 16 minutes.
5. Cool the dessert well and cut into bars.

Nutrition: calories 298, fat 29.8, fiber 3.5, carbs 6.2, protein 4.1

Keto Blondies

Prep time: 10 minutes
Cooking time: 15 minutes
Servings: 2

Ingredients:
- 1 egg, beaten
- 1 tablespoon almond butter
- ½ teaspoon baking powder
- 1 teaspoon lime juice
- ½ teaspoon vanilla extract
- 1 teaspoon Splenda
- 2 tablespoons almond flour

Directions:
1. Put all ingredients in the mixer bowl and mix until smooth.
2. Pour the mixture in the air fryer basket, flatten gently, and cook at 375F for 15 minutes.
3. Then cut the cooked dessert into servings.

Nutrition: calories 138, fat 10.1, fiber 1.6, carbs 6.4, protein 6

Chocolate Cream

Preparation time: 10 minutes
Cooking time: 15 minutes
Servings: 3

Ingredients:
- 1 oz dark chocolate, chopped
- 1 cup coconut cream
- 1 teaspoon vanilla extract

- 1 tablespoon Erythritol

Directions:
1. Pour coconut cream in the air fryer.
2. Add chocolate, vanilla extract, and Erythritol.
3. Cook the chocolate cream for 15 minutes at 360F. Stir the liquid from time to time during cooking.

Nutrition: calories 236, fat 21.9, fiber 2, carbs 10.3, protein 2.6

Pecan Nutella

Prep time: 20 minutes
Cooking time: 5 minutes
Servings: 4

Ingredients:
- 4 pecans, chopped
- 5 teaspoons butter, softened
- ½ teaspoon vanilla extract
- 1 tablespoon Splenda
- 1 teaspoon of cocoa powder

Directions:
1. Put all ingredients in the air fryer and stir gently.
2. Cook the mixture at 400F for 5 minutes.
3. Then transfer the mixture in the serving bowl and refrigerate for 15-20 minutes before serving.

Nutrition: calories 157, fat 14.8, fiber 1.6, carbs 5.3, protein 1.6

Ricotta Cookies

Preparation time: 15 minutes
Cooking time: 12 minutes
Servings: 6

Ingredients:
- 1 teaspoon vanilla extract
- 1 cup ricotta cheese
- 1 cup coconut flour
- 1 egg, beaten
- 2 tablespoons swerve

Directions:
1. Mix coconut flour with vanilla extract, ricotta cheese, egg, and swerve.
2. Knead the dough and make cookies.
3. Put the cookies in the air fryer and cook at 365F for 12 minutes.

Nutrition: calories 150, fat 6, fiber 8, carbs 15.6, protein 8.3

Cream Cheese Pie

Prep time: 15 minutes
Cooking time: 30 minutes
Servings: 6

Ingredients:
- 2 eggs, beaten
- 6 tablespoons almond flour
- ½ teaspoon vanilla extract
- 6 tablespoons cream cheese
- ½ teaspoon baking powder
- 1 teaspoon apple cider vinegar
- ½ teaspoon ground cinnamon
- 3 tablespoons Erythritol
- 1 tablespoon coconut oil, melted

Directions:
1. Brush the baking pan with coconut oil.
2. Then mix eggs with almond flour, vanilla extract, cream cheese, baking powder, apple cider vinegar, ground cinnamon, and Erythritol.
3. Blend the mixture until smooth and pour it in the baking pan.

4. Cook the pie in the air fryer at 350F for 30 minutes.
5. Then cool the cooked pie well.

Nutrition: calories 120, fat 10.6, fiber 0.9, carbs 2.3, protein 4.1

Greece Style Cake

Preparation time: 10 minutes
Cooking time: 30 minutes
Servings: 12

Ingredients:
- 6 eggs, beaten
- 1 teaspoon vanilla extract
- 1 teaspoon baking powder
- 2 cups almond flour
- 4 tablespoons Erythritol
- 1 cup Plain yogurt

Directions:
1. Mix all ingredients in the mixing bowl.
2. Then pour the mixture in the air fryer and flatten it gently.
3. Cook the cake at 350F for 30 minutes.

Nutrition: calories 159, fat 11.3, fiber 2, carbs 5.9, protein 7.9

Pecan Cobbler

Prep time: 15 minutes
Cooking time: 30 minutes
Servings: 4

Ingredients:
- ¼ cup coconut cream
- 1 egg, beaten
- ½ cup coconut flour
- 1 teaspoon vanilla extract
- 2 tablespoons coconut oil, softened
- 3 pecans, chopped

Directions:
1. Mix coconut oil with pecans and put the mixture in the air fryer. Flatten the mixture gently.
2. In the mixing bowl, mix coconut cream with egg, coconut flour, and vanilla extract.
3. Put the mixture over the pecans, flatten it gently and cook at 350F for 30 minutes.
4. Cool the cooked meal and transfer in the plates.

Nutrition: calories 245, fat 20.5, fiber 7.5, carbs 12.5, protein 4.8

Cocoa Pudding

Preparation time: 10 minutes
Cooking time: 20 minutes
Servings: 8

Ingredients:
- 2 cups ricotta cheese
- 2 tablespoons coconut flour
- 3 tablespoons Splenda
- 3 eggs, beaten
- 1 tablespoon vanilla extract
- ½ cup coconut cream
- 1 tablespoon cocoa powder

Directions:
1. Whisk the coconut cream with cocoa powder.
2. Then add eggs, Splenda, ricotta cheese, and coconut flour.
3. Mix the mixture until smooth and pour in the air fryer.
4. Cook the pudding at 350F for 20 minutes. Stir the pudding every 5 minutes during cooking.

Nutrition: calories 180, fat 10.4, fiber 1.3, carbs 10.5, protein 9.9

Lemon Biscotti

Prep time: 15 minutes
Cooking time: 40 minutes
Servings: 6

Ingredients:
- 2 oz almonds, chopped
- 2 tablespoons coconut oil
- 2 eggs, beaten
- 1 teaspoon vanilla extract
- 1 cup coconut flour
- 1 teaspoon lemon zest, grated
- ½ teaspoon baking powder
- 1 teaspoon lemon juice
- ¼ cup coconut cream
- 1 teaspoon sesame oil
- 3 tablespoons Erythritol

Directions:
1. Mix all ingredients in the mixing bowl.
2. Then knead the dough and put in the air fryer basket.
3. Cook the dough for 38 minutes at 375F.
4. Then slice the dough into biscotti and cook at 400F for 2 minutes more.

Nutrition: calories 227, fat 15.9, fiber 9.4, carbs 16.4, protein 6.8

Chia Pie

Preparation time: 10 minutes
Cooking time: 30 minutes
Servings: 8

Ingredients:
- 1 cup almond flour
- 2 tablespoons chia seeds
- 4 eggs, beaten
- 4 tablespoons Erythritol
- 1 teaspoon vanilla extract
- 2 tablespoons coconut oil, melted

Directions:
1. Brush the air fryer basket with coconut oil.
2. Then mix almond flour with chia seeds, eggs, vanilla extract, and Erythritol.
3. Put the mixture in the air fryer basket, flatten it in the shape of the pie and cook at 365F for 30 minutes.

Nutrition: calories 164, fat 13.3, fiber 2.7, carbs 4.7, protein 6.4

Ricotta Muffins

Prep time: 15 minutes
Cooking time: 11 minutes
Servings: 4

Ingredients:
- 4 teaspoons ricotta cheese
- 1 egg, beaten
- ½ teaspoon baking powder
- 1 teaspoon vanilla extract
- 8 teaspoons coconut flour
- 3 tablespoons coconut cream
- 2 teaspoons Erythritol
- Cooking spray

Directions:
1. Spray the muffin molds with cooking spray.
2. Then mix all ingredients in the mixing bowl.
3. When you get a smooth batter, pour it in the muffin molds and place in the air fryer basket.
4. Cook the muffins at 365F for 11 minutes.

Nutrition: calories 72, fat 4.7, fiber 2.3, carbs 4.7, protein 2.9

Sweet Baked Avocado

Preparation time: 5 minutes
Cooking time: 20 minutes
Servings: 2

Ingredients:
- 1 avocado, pitted, halved
- 2 teaspoons Erythritol
- 1 teaspoon vanilla extract
- 2 teaspoons butter

Directions:
1. Sprinkle the avocado halves with Erythritol, vanilla extract, and butter.
2. Put the avocado halves in the air fryer and cook at 350F for 20 minutes.

Nutrition: calories 245, fat 23.4, fiber 6.7, carbs 8.9, protein 2

Rhubarb Pie

Prep time: 15 minutes
Cooking time: 20 minutes
Servings: 6

Ingredients:
- 4 oz rhubarb, chopped
- ¼ cup coconut cream
- 1 teaspoon vanilla extract
- ¼ cup Erythritol
- 1 cup coconut flour
- 1 egg, beaten
- 4 tablespoons coconut oil, softened

Directions:
1. Mix coconut cream with vanilla extract, Erythritol, coconut flour, egg, and coconut oil.
2. When the mixture is smooth, add rhubarb and stir gently.
3. Pour the mixture in the air fryer and cook the pie at 375F for 20 minutes.
4. Cool the cooked pie and cut into servings.

Nutrition: calories 198, fat 14.2, fiber 8.6, carbs 14.9, protein 4

Lemon Pie

Preparation time: 10 minutes
Cooking time: 35 minutes
Servings: 6

Ingredients:
- 1 cup coconut flour
- ½ lemon, sliced
- ¼ cup heavy cream
- 2 eggs, beaten
- 2 tablespoons Erythritol
- 1 teaspoon baking powder
- Cooking spray

Directions:
1. Spray the air fryer basket with cooking spray.
2. Then line the bottom of the air fryer with lemon.
3. In the mixing bowl, mix coconut flour with heavy cream, eggs, Erythritol, and baking powder.
4. Pour the batter over the lemons and cook the pie at 365f for 35 minutes.

Nutrition: calories 120, fat 5.3, fiber 8.2, carbs 14.4, protein 4.7

Keto Sponge

Prep time: 10 minutes
Cooking time: 30 minutes
Servings: 6

Ingredients:
- 2 cups coconut flour
- 5 eggs, beaten
- ½ cup Erythritol
- 1 teaspoon baking powder
- 1 teaspoon vanilla extract

- Cooking spray

Directions:
1. Whisk the coconut flour with eggs, Erythritol, baking powder, and vanilla extract.
2. Spray the baking pan with cooking spray and pour the coconut flour mixture inside.
3. Put the pan in the air fryer basket and cook at 355F for 30 minutes.

Nutrition: calories 75, fat 4.3, fiber 1.7, carbs 3.4, protein 5.3

Baked Cantaloupe

Preparation time: 10 minutes
Cooking time: 10 minutes
Servings: 2

Ingredients:
- 1 cup cantaloupe, chopped
- 1 teaspoon vanilla extract
- 1 tablespoon Erythritol
- 1 teaspoon olive oil

Directions:
1. Put the cantaloupe in the air fryer basket and sprinkle with vanilla extract, Erythritol, and olive oil.
2. Cook the dessert at 375F for 10 minutes.

Nutrition: calories 53, fat 2.5, fiber 0.7, carbs 6.6, protein 0.7

Sweet Carambola Chips

Prep time: 10 minutes
Cooking time: 50 minutes
Servings: 6

Ingredients:
- 10 oz carambola, sliced

- 1 teaspoon coconut oil, melted
- 1 tablespoon Erythritol

Directions:
1. Mix carambola with coconut oil and Erythritol.
2. Then put it in the air fryer and cook at 340F for 50 minutes. Shake the carambola slices every 5 minutes.

Nutrition: calories 21, fat 0.9, fiber 1.3, carbs 3.2, protein 0.5

Blueberries Muffins

Preparation time: 10 minutes
Cooking time: 20 minutes
Servings: 6

Ingredients:
- 2 teaspoons blueberries
- 1 teaspoon baking powder
- 4 tablespoons coconut flour
- 4 tablespoons coconut oil, softened
- 3 tablespoons Erythritol

Directions:
1. Put all ingredients in the mixing bowl and mix until smooth.
2. Then pour the mixture in the muffin molds.
3. Place the muffin molds in the air fryer basket and cook at 350F for 20 minutes.

Nutrition: calories 100, fat 9.6, fiber 2, carbs 9.9, protein 0.7

Cinnamon Plum Halves

Prep time: 5 minutes
Cooking time: 10 minutes
Servings: 4

Ingredients:

- 4 plums, pitted, halved
- 1 teaspoon ground cinnamon
- 1 teaspoon coconut oil, melted

Directions:
1. Put the plum halves in the air fryer basket in one layer.

2. Then sprinkle them with ground cinnamon and coconut oil.
3. Cook the plums at 360F for 10 minutes.

Nutrition: calories 41, fat 1.3, fiber 1.2, carbs 8.5, protein 0.5

Measurement Conversion Charts

Measurement

Cup	Ounces	Milliliters	Tablespoons
8 cups	64 oz	1895 ml	128
6 cups	48 oz	1420 ml	96
5 cups	40 oz	1180 ml	80
4 cups	32 oz	960 ml	64
2 cups	16 oz	480 ml	32
1 cup	8 oz	240 ml	16
3/4 cup	6 oz	177 ml	12
2/3 cup	5 oz	158 ml	11
1/2 cup	4 oz	118 ml	8
3/8 cup	3 oz	90 ml	6
1/3 cup	2.5 oz	79 ml	5.5
1/4 cup	2 oz	59 ml	4
1/8 cup	1 oz	30 ml	3
1/16 cup	1/2 oz	15 ml	1

Weight

Imperial	Metric
1/2 oz	15 g
1 oz	29 g
2 oz	57 g
3 oz	85 g
4 oz	113 g
5 oz	141 g
6 oz	170 g
8 oz	227 g
10 oz	283 g
12 oz	340 g
13 oz	369 g
14 oz	397 g
15 oz	425 g
1 lb	453 g

Temperature

Fahrenheit	Celsius
100 °F	37 °C
150 °F	65 °C
200 °F	93 °C
250 °F	121 °C
300 °F	150 °C
325 °F	160 °C
350 °F	180 °C
375 °F	190 °C
400 °F	200 °C
425 °F	220 °C
450 °F	230 °C
500 °F	260 °C
525 °F	274 °C
550 °F	288 °C

CPSIA information can be obtained
at www.ICGtesting.com
Printed in the USA
BVHW051539141021
618952BV00004B/216